THE ECONOMICS OF INFORMATION TECHNOLOGY

Also by Paul Jowett

PARTY STRATEGIES IN BRITAIN (*with David Butler*)

The Economics of Information Technology

Paul Jowett
Research Associate of Templeton College, Oxford

and

Margaret Rothwell
Lecturer in Economics, Oxford Polytechnic

St. Martin's Press   New York

© Paul Jowett and Margaret Rothwell, 1986

All rights reserved. For information, write:
Scholarly & Reference Division,
St. Martin's Press, Inc., 175 Fifth Avenue, New York, NY 10010

First published in the United States of America in 1986

Printed in Great Britain

ISBN 0–312–23434–1

Library of Congress Cataloging-in-Publication Data
Jowett, Paul.
The economics of information technology.
Bibliography: p.
Includes index.
1. Computer industry. 2. Telecommunication
equipment industry. I. Rothwell, Margaret. II. Title.
HD9696 C62J68 1986   338.4'7004   86–1268
ISBN 0–312–23434–1

Contents

List of Illustrations

List of Figures

List of Tables

Preface

This book analyses the development of Information Technology (IT) at both the microeconomic and macroeconomic level. At the microeconomic level, individual firms, universities and research laboratories in Britain, Europe, the USA and Japan are the principal focus of attention, whereas, at the macroeconomic level, investigations are made and comparisons drawn between the countries' differing national efforts and the key role their governments have played in stimulating these. Whilst the scope of this book is broad, its objective is specific: to identify the principal economic determinants of success for companies and countries working in the field of IT, and to explain why certain companies and countries have performed better at times than others.

The reasons for writing a book on the economics of IT are many. The most obvious is that IT has become a major new, fiercely competitive, and rapidly changing world industry – one which has applications in all three traditional economic sectors (primary, secondary and tertiary), one which almost every developed (and to a certain extent underdeveloped) nation has sought to enter, and one whose strategic potential is immense. This in itself makes the IT industry a worthy subject for economic analysis.

Writing a book on such a broad and all-encompassing subject has not been easy. Because of the lack of any existing competent introduction to the subject, this book has a distinctly historical slant. Only by reviewing the origins and subsequent development of this new industry can one discern trends on the basis of which future projections about the industry's structure and strategic importance can be made. This book does not offer a complete history of the economics of IT. What it does is to select particular examples of the development of IT, from various countries, which illustrate most clearly the trends and determinants of success at that time. Thus, the reader is provided not with an historical summary, devoid of any economic theory, but with a stimulating and dynamic applied economic analysis of an exciting industry.

No attempt has been made to relate this applied analysis directly to existing economic theory, and the reasons for this are twofold. Firstly, the traditional economic theory of entry barriers, collusion between rivals and the effect of technical change on market structure, neither accurately or adequately describes the dynamic IT industry. Secondly, the modification of existing, and development of new, theories, although of academic interest and importance, lies beyond the scope and objectives of this book, which is intended to appeal to as large an audience as possible, including non-specialists. In addition, no attempt has been made to investigate the present and future impact of IT on other sectors of the economy, since a task as difficult and complex as this would, in itself, provide ample scope for a second book.

Acknowledgements

We would like to thank the London Business School and Oxford Polytechnic for providing us with the time and institutional support to write this book. In the course of our work we have been helped by many people in the IT industry, government and academia who have given generously of their time in allowing us to interview them. Several people also took time to read and comment upon chapters, and we would like to thank the following in particular: Professor Tony Hoare, Professor Roger Needham, Richard Ennals, Tim Walker, Graham Ashe, John Hendry, Richard Nobbs, and Stuart MacDonald. We also would like to express our thanks to those who have given permission to reproduce the copyright material in the book.

We are also very grateful to Mrs Kathleen Rothwell, who diligently proof-read the book for us. Any errors which remain are, of course, our own.

Oxford
April 1986

PAUL JOWETT
MARGARET ROTHWELL

Abbreviations and Acronyms

ACARD	Advisory Council on Applied Research and Development
AI	Artificial Intelligence
AT&T	American Telephone and Telegraph
BAe	British Aerospace
BT	British Telecom
BTG	British Technology Group
CADDIA	Cooperation in Automation of Data and Documentation for Imports/Exports and Agriculture
CD – ROM	Compact Disk – Read Only Memory
CEPT	Conférence Européene des Administrations des Postes et des Télecommunications
CGR	Compagnie Générale de Radiologie
CSA	Computer Services Association (UK)
DARPA	Defence Advanced Research Projects Agency (USA)
DBS	Direct Broadcasting by Satellite
DEC	Digital Equipment Corporation (USA)
DES	Department of Education and Science (UK)
DM	Deutsche Mark
DoD	Department of Defense (USA)
DoI	Department of Industry, pre-1983 (UK)
DTI	Department of Trade and Industry, post-1983 (UK)
ECU	European Currency Unit
EEC	European Economic Community
ESPRIT	European Strategic Programme of Research and Development in Information Technology
ETL	Electrotechnical Laboratory (Japan)
FGCS	Fifth Generation Computer Society (Japan)
GEC	General Electric Company (UK)
GLC	Greater London Council
IBM	International Business Machines (USA)
IC	Integrated Circuit
ICL	International Computers Limited (UK)
ICOT	Institute for Fifth Generation Computer Technology (Japan)
ICT	International Computers and Tabulators (UK)
IKBS	Intelligent Knowledge Based Systems
IPR	Intellectual Property Rights
IRC	Industrial Reorganisation Corporation (UK)
IT	Information Technology

ITT	International Telephone and Telegraph
JECC	Japanese Electronics and Computer Company
JEIDA	Japanese Electronics Industry Development Association
JVC	Victor Company of Japan (subsidiary of Matsushita)
K	1000 bits
LSE	London School of Economics
MCC	Microelectronics and Computer Technology Corporation
MEP	Member of the European Parliament
MISP	Microelectronics Industry Support Programme
MIT	Massachusetts Institute of Technology
MITI	Ministry of International Trade and Industry (Japan)
MMI	Man Machine Interface
MoD	Ministry of Defence (UK)
NCR	National Cash Register (USA)
NEB	National Enterprise Board (UK)
NEC	Nippon Electric Company (Japan)
NEDC	National Economic Development Council (UK)
NTT	Nippon Telephone and Telegraph (Japan)
PABX	Private Branch Exchange
PIPS	Pattern Information Processing Project (Japan)
PROLOG	AI Programming Language
QC	Queen's Counsel
R&D	Research and Development
RAM	Random Access Memory
RCA	Radio Corporation of America
SIA	Semiconductor Industry Association (USA)
SERC	Science and Engineering Research Council (UK)
SNA	Systems Interconnect Architecture
SRC	Semiconductor Research Cooperative (USA)
STARS	Software Technology for Adaptable and Reliable Systems (USA)
STC	Standard Telephone and Cable (UK)
STELLA	High Speed Data Transmission Project (EEC)
UK	United Kingdom
US(A)	United States (of America)
VCR	Video Cassette Recorder
VHS	JVC's VCR system
VHSIC	Very High Speed Integrated Circuit
VLSI	Very Large Scale Integration

Introduction

The IT industry eludes precise definition. The Department of Trade and Industry (DTI) spent a difficult and fruitless year in 1983 wrestling with this problem, and were still searching for an accurate and comprehensive description in 1985.

For the purposes of this book, the IT industry may be thought of as embracing telecommunications (telephones, switches, exchanges, cables, satellites and broadcasting), on the one hand, and computers, on the other. Both have a history stretching back to the second half of the nineteenth century, but the differences in the technology which they initially used made any association of the two industries unlikely in the early years of their development.

The convergence of the two industries did not begin until after the Second World War, when, largely due to the research efforts of British and American universities, computers became data-processing as opposed to merely business calculating machines, and multifunctional compatible electronic components, common to both industries, were developed to replace the single-function non-compatible type that had previously been used (see Figure 1). In addition, both industries required technical expertise in electromechanical (and later electronic) equipment, both relied heavily on government R&D contracts and orders, and both had considerable experience of working on costly long-term projects for a limited number of customers. Hence, not only was it the case that the technology used by the two industries was converging, but also the economic and political environment in which they operated was becoming increasingly similar.

However, despite these developments, instances of telecommunications and computing being used together were few and far between before the onset of the 1970s. The main commercial function of the two in the 1960s was for use in computer bureaux, where a client would have a terminal in his business linked by a telephone line to a computer owned by the bureau. The main contribution of telecommunications to computing in the 1960s was therefore to increase computers' accessibility to companies which could not afford their own. During the 1970s, as a consequence of

1

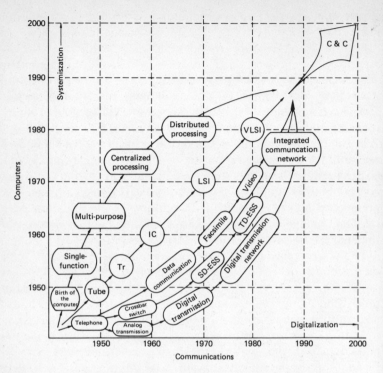

Figure 1   The convergence of computers and communications
Source: Dr K. Kobayashi, 'Man and C & C: Concepts and Perspectives',
International Institute of Communications Annual Conference, 1982.

increasing economies of scale in production and further technological developments, the cost and size of computers dropped
dramatically, and many companies that had previously used a
bureau service bought their own computer. As computers became
cheaper and more ubiquitous, a thriving software industry began
to grow (often from the shells of the computer service bureaux
which had provided programming facilities in the 1960s). By the
1980s, following the introduction of the microcomputer, the need
for a centralized computing system based on a data-processing
department of experienced programmers began to wane, and this,
together with the rapid development of 'user-friendly' software,

meant that the vision of a computer age, in which information would be the new wealth of nations, was becoming a reality.

With a rapid growth in the number of mini- and micro-computers (see Figure 2) it became increasingly apparent that there were considerable advantages to be reaped if they could be made compatible and linked to a common network. For this to be possible, developments had to be made in the interface of many different machines, and complicated networking systems devised to allow the right information to go to the right terminal in a form that could be understood by the machine. In addition, it was realized that if the scale of networking could be increased, using telephone lines and satellites, it would be possible to develop global computer communication systems. By the early 1980s such a system had been partially developed, and was already revolutionizing the operations of some multinational corporations. On a

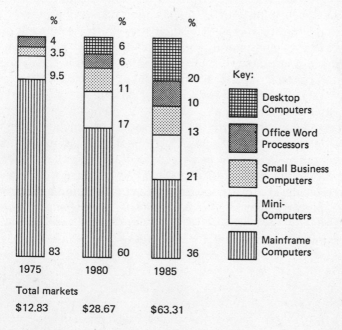

Figure 2 World-wide shipments by US manufacturers, billions of dollars
Source: International Data Corporation, 1985.

smaller scale, at the local level, home-banking systems were being introduced, via British Telecom's Prestel, and one of the major stimuli behind the laying of cable was not only to make possible extra television channels but also to provide interactive communicative systems (rivalling the telephone network) for homes.

The potential of all these developments is clearly very great, and has been recognized at the level of both companies and the government. Particularly from the company perspective, such international networks bring sellers closer to the market, and can allow head offices to keep tight control over their branches, even when these are situated in a different country. Furthermore, as developments in computing continue, the range of computer services available will increase, particularly once one is able to talk directly to computers, in any language, and receive spoken replies.

On the side of government, because of their implications for, among other things, national defence, it is apparent that certain developments within the IT industry, both present and future, are (and will be) of immense strategic importance. Consequently, this raises the thorny issue of the role, if any, which government policy ought to play in promoting and protecting military applications. In addition, if information is to be a key ingredient in the recipe for future economic success, the government may have an important and vital role to play in fostering an environment in which the IT industry can survive and command a dominant position in a fiercely competitive market. This book, by tracing the global development of the IT industry from its origins to the recent international struggle to construct the world's first Fifth Generation Computer, attempts to provide the reader not only with a coherent analysis of the economic forces determining success in this rapidly changing market but also with an insight into the more general and controversial issue of whether or not government intervention in this market is either desirable or necessary.

1 Background to the Information Technology Race

This chapter reviews and evaluates the economic, political and geographical development of IT, examining the crucial issue of the appropriate role of the government, and analysing the global strategies of companies participating in the IT race between 1945 and 1980. Consequently, industrial development and government policies in the USA, Japan and Britain are the principal focus of attention.

We begin this chapter by identifying the changes which have taken place throughout the post-war period, in terms of technological supremity and leadership, within the computer industries of the USA, Japan and Britain. This is followed by an examination of, on the one hand, the markets for which the computers of these three countries were destined, and, on the other, the characteristics of supplier companies. We then proceed to review, firstly, certain key technological developments that have occurred within the semiconductor industry, and their effects upon companies engaged in semiconductor production, and, secondly, the impact of major post-war developments upon the telecommunications industries of the USA, Japan and Britain. The final section of this chapter investigates the effects government policies have had upon IT industries in general, and highlights additional factors which it is felt might have caused, or have been at least partially responsible for, discrepancies in the development of American, Japanese and British IT companies.

Although, in the immediate post-war period, both the University of Pennsylvania in the USA and the universities of Cambridge and Manchester in Britain were centres of computer expertise, by 1960 the USA had moved far ahead in commercial exploitation, and by the beginning of the 1970s the UK was not only heavily dependent upon components, peripherals and technology imported from the USA but was also being further threatened by the Japanese economic and technological miracle.

Following the devastation of the Second World War, the Japanese were initially dependent upon technology transfers from the USA. However, by the 1960s they were already beginning to show signs of scientific and technological excellence in certain IT areas, and by the late 1970s and early 1980s it was argued that Japan had achieved technological parity with, perhaps even superiority over, America.

At the beginning of 1980 Japan and the USA were considered to be occupying technologically equivalent positions in the computer market. Whilst the Americans had the edge in software, the Japanese were clearly in a situation of competitive superiority in the production of microelectronic components. By this time both the UK and Europe had become technological laggards, and consequently were extremely ill-placed to reap the benefits of future IT developments (see Figure 3).

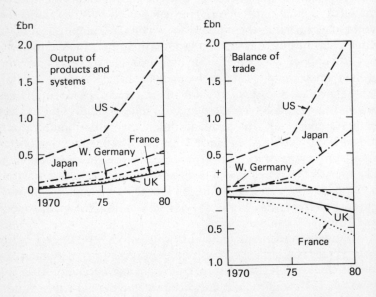

Figure 3   IT: output of products and systems, and balance of trade
Source: MITI, Electronic Policy Division, 1980.

The original computers developed during and immediately after the Second World War were designed for military applications. In the USA, throughout the period 1945–85, not only was this defence-oriented competence continually improved, but also, from the 1950s onwards, a rapidly expanding commercial sector of the computer market began to develop, particularly in the sphere of data processing. (For a break-down of American semiconductor sales by end-use segment, see Figure 4.) In Britain, however, despite the fact that in the post-war period this commercial side of the market was to become the most rapidly expanding, existing computer knowledge and expertise remained largely within electronics firms concentrating on military applications which were ill-equipped to market on the commercial side, and consequently, as the demand for commercial computers increased, this was met by American suppliers rather than British. As British defence expenditure continued to increase in the early 1980s, the incentive for domestic producers to serve military computing needs rather than commercial requirements was accentuated, such that by 1985 the bulk of Britain's domestic computing capacity was concentrated upon military applications. In Japan, by contrast, largely as a consequence of demilitarization after her defeat in 1945 and the continuation of a policy of low defence expenditure, the post-war

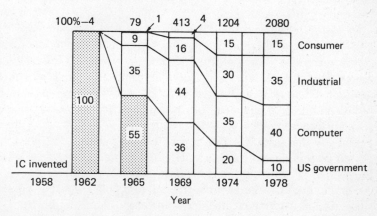

Figure 4   Percentage values of American IC sales by end-use segment, millions of dollars

development of computing was almost entirely in the commercial, non-military, sector.

Hence, there were considerable differences between Japan, the USA and Britain in the factors that affected and determined the direction of development in the computer industry. In the USA, although initially concerned with military applications, the computer industry was quick to realize the tremendous market potential offered by commercial applications, and responded effectively. Japan's particular historical circumstances resulted in her focusing, with phenomenal success, on the commercial side of the computer market. In the UK the loss of commercial markets to the fiercely competitive Japanese and American producers, combined with government defence expenditure policies, resulted in an almost total concentration upon military applications.

Besides this, there were a number of other important differences in the development of the computer industry between the USA, Britain and Japan. In the USA, with the exception of IBM, the only American company to have taken vertical integration to its limits, the computer industry was divided into a number of specialist companies manufacturing various components, peripherals and software, and a smaller but growing number of companies assembling final computer products. By contrast, IBM not only made a large proportion of its own integrated circuits and peripherals but also had a world-wide distribution network second to none.

In Japan, however, the vertically integrated company was the norm, with many Japanese computer companies making their own electronic components, peripherals and software, as well as being responsible for distributing and marketing the final computer product. In contrast, in the UK and Europe there were, at various points in time, a diversity of vertically integrated and smaller specialist companies.

One of the principal differences between the vertically integrated companies of the USA, UK and Japan, is in the markets they serve. Following logically from a previous point, Japanese companies tend to be exclusively commercially oriented, possessing large consumer electronics divisions for the manufacture of hi-fis, televisions etc., whereas the American companies, although selling to both the military and commercial domains, have tended to be specialist computer producers as a consequence of their early domination of the world computer market. Although in Britain it is difficult to identify a typical vertically integrated company, the largest and most successful companies are those serving the military market, i.e. GEC, Plessey, Racal and Ferranti, none of which sells mass-produced commercial data-processing machines. ICL, Britain's only commercial mainframe – and mini-computer company, through a policy in the 1980s of enlarging the proportion of components and peripherals brought from outsiders, has become increasingly less vertically integrated. On the other hand, Thorn EMI, which was created through the merger of an essentially military electronics company (EMI) and a consumer electronics company (Thorn), is perhaps the only vertically integrated British electronics company that is serving both the commercial and military computer sectors. (Because of financial troubles, the reverse has happened to West Germany's AEG-Telefunken, which was forced to sell off its unprofitable consumer electronics division in 1982.) In Europe the largest vertically integrated electronics company manufacturing computers is Philips, which, like its Japanese counterparts, tends to specialize in commercial rather than military applications.

The development of the semiconductor industry has followed a similar pattern to that of the computer industry. The first semiconductor (the transistor), developed in the Bell Laboratories in 1946, quickly replaced the valve as the principal component for computers, and by the mid-1960s the market for semiconductors had become fiercely competitive. Companies unable to keep pace with technological change were in many cases bought by large electronics companies, e.g. Philips acquired Signetics, Commodore bought Mos Technology, Japan's NEC bought Electronic Arrays, and Schlumberger took over Fairchild. Many of the semiconductor companies chose to specialize in the components they produced, and, consequently, by the mid-1970s, Intel had become the market leader in microprocessors, while Mostek achieved pre-eminence in the memory business.

The development of semiconductors in Europe began several steps behind America, and was confined largely to the major electronics companies. The British and European companies tended to concentrate their efforts on making small runs of custom and semi-custom semiconductors for aircraft and weapon systems, and were not significant suppliers of mass-produced components for other electronic products.

In Japan there was a parallel development in both semiconductors and computers from the 1960s onwards. After having occupied a relatively insignificant position in the microelectronic components market in the 1960s and early 1970s, Japan emerged at the end of the 1970s as the world's leading supplier of mass-produced memory chips, having clearly beaten America in the race to develop the 128K and 256K RAM chips (see Abbreviations and acronyms for an explanation of terms). The vast majority of Japanese chips were manufactured by vertically integrated computer and consumer electronics companies, and were used in the production of consumer electronics products.

While the computer and semiconductor industries developed at a similar pace, and were driven largely by technological advances in the world market, this was not, for a number of reasons, the case in the telecommunications industry. Because the provision of telecommunications was a virtual monopoly in all three continents, with national telecommunications authorities working in close conjunction with equipment suppliers, the telecommunications market was not driven by the type of fierce, inter-company innovation-inducing competition. It was not until the late 1960s and early 1970s that pressure for the liberalization of telecommunications surfaced. The American market was the first to succumb, with the Carterphone decision in 1969, which allowed users to connect any telephone of their choice into the national network. The liberalization of the American system, which eventually resulted in the divestiture of American Telephone and Telegraph (AT&T) in 1982, made the American telecommunications industry more competitive and innovative, and, consequently, by the beginning of 1980, American telecommunications equipment was further advanced than that in any other country, being capable of interfacing and merging with computer products. The British also attempted to open up their market for the supply of telecommunications equipment in the 1970s and 1980s, culminating in the privatization of British Telecom in 1985. The Japanese, although having a telecommunications agency far less vertically integrated than their British and American counterparts, also followed a similar course, liberalizing NTT on 1 April 1985.

Throughout the post-war period the governments of the USA, Britain and Japan pursued, with different degrees of success, various policies designed to encourage and foster the development of national IT companies. There were five major instruments available to these governments: R&D support, purchasing policies, regulations, policies aimed at influencing industry structure, and, finally, the provision of infrastructure assistance. All these measures have been used in varying degrees by the governments of the USA, UK and Japan.

R&D support includes government grants for specific research projects, cost-plus contracts, and the subsidization of joint development projects. Purchasing policy essentially refers to favourable arrangements devised by the government for the purchase of products from domestic companies. Regulation covers the raising or lowering of tariff boundaries, the introduction or withdrawal of import quotas, and the granting and breaking up of monopolies. Attempts to influence industry structure include rationalization via the encouragement of acquisitions and mergers; state investment, either directly or via a government agency; and the privatization of companies either wholly or partly state-owned. Infrastructural support includes the establishment of agencies to assist with the introduction of advanced technology, the development of suitable educational courses, the encouragement of forums for discussion, together with aid for research and the overseas marketing of products.

Encouraged by infrastructural government aid, the immediate post-war development of computers occurred principally in American and British universities. However, it was the Americans who first successfully used purchasing policies to enhance rapid growth of domestic computer companies and race ahead of Britain. Between 1950 and 1958 IBM received $396m and Univac $702m in federal contracts. By contrast, only a handful of government orders for computers were placed with British companies during the same period.

The government policy that most dramatically affected and influenced the development of the American IT industry, on a world-wide as well as national basis, was the system of R&D support grants, totalling $900m between 1958 and 1974, which were given to semiconductor firms for the development of miniaturized electronic components for use in both weapon systems and the space progamme, and which were clearly instrumental in the development of the first integrated circuits by Texas Instruments and Fairchild in 1961. (For details of public support for the US IT industry see Table 1.)

The main support for the British electronics industry in the immediate post-war period was via the Post Office, which in 1956 sponsored the creation of the Joint Electronics Research Committee to coordinate the research efforts of British companies manufacturing telephone exchanges. At the end of the 1950s and beginning of the 1960s, British companies, with the aid of government development contracts, produced the first electronic exchange, a prototype of which was installed at Highgate Wood. However, although the technology behind this exchange was extremely advanced, its manufacture proved to be totally uneconomic, and, at a time when exchanges were heavily in demand, the decision was made in 1963 to opt for less sophisticated reed relay technology systems.

The problem facing telecommunications companies in Britain was that the communication network was, at this time, being used

Table 1 Public policy towards information technology in the USA

Year(s)	Title	Value	Notes
1950–8	Federal computer contracts	$1098m	$702m for Univac, $396m for IBM
1958–74	R&D support for semi-conductors	$900m	Space programme and weapons development
1984–90	STARS	$5m in 1984	Integrated software tools
1984–94	Strategic computing	$1bn	Defence project
1984–94	Space station	$8bn	Hardware and software development

by the Treasury as a means of raising revenue to cross-subsidize the postal service, which, although set up as a corporation in 1961, still remained closely tied by Treasury strings. This ultimately resulted in the network being starved of essential capital and unable to replace ageing exchanges.

In 1961 the National Economic Development Council (NEDC) was created. It later became an important forum via which electronics companies could lobby the government for support, but it was not until the Labour victory of 1964, which brought Harold Wilson to power, that a more constructive policy for electronics began to develop. Soon after the election the Ministry of Technology and the Industrial Reorganisation Corporation (IRC) were set up, and they were both to play an influential role in the electronics industry. A government preferential procurement policy towards domestic producers began in 1965, and in 1968, Tony Benn, as the Minister of Technology, intervened to encourage rationalization within the computer and telecommunication industries. English Electric was persuaded to merge its DP computer activity with International Computers and Tabulators (ICT) to form International Computers Ltd (ICL), in which the government made an investment of 10.5 per cent of the total equity, in addition to substantial investments made (albeit temporarily) by GEC and Plessey.

From its creation in 1968 until its financial collapse in 1981 and subsequent merger with STC in 1984, ICL was the spearhead of the government's computer policy. Between 1968 and 1973 ICL was given £7m in R&D grants and £40m in loans (which it was later able to avoid repaying). (A summary of the other forms of support offered by the British government during this period is shown in Table 2.) Although the government formalized its preferential procurement policy towards purchasing ICL computers, such that by 1972 two-thirds of all government contracts were taken by ICL, a new element of competition was introduced in telecommunication supplies, following the decision of the government in 1969 not to renew the agreement that had existed between the Post Office and certain telecommunication suppliers, which had given these suppliers a degree of monopoly power. This action had been provoked largely by the refusal of established suppliers to make the investment necessary to produce equipment requested

Table 2 Public policy towards information technology in the UK

Year(s)	Title	Value	Notes
1968	Industry restructuring	10.5 per cent of equity in ICL	Government-backed merger of ICT and English Electric's DP Department
1968–73	R&D grants for ICL, unrepaid loans	£7m £40m	Government funds for development of independent technology
1973–82	Software Product Scheme	£9m	25–30 per cent grants to costs of developing package software
1973–8	Microeclectronics Support Scheme	£10m	Support for domestic microelectronics firms
1973–8	Advanced Computer Technology Project	£2m pa $5m pa	Support for domestic semiconductor firms
1976	Component Industry Scheme	£5m $9m	Support for domestic components firms
1978	Microelectronics Industry Support Scheme (MISP)	£55m $110m	50 per cent grants to R&D and 25 per cent to cost of productive investments
1978–81	Microprocessor Application Programme	£41m $73m	For diffusion of microelectronic applications in industry
1978	Creation of INMOS	£50m $100m	NEB sponsored, to create memory device firm in Britain
1979	Microelectronics in Education Programme	£10m $18m	For diffusion of microelectronic applications in schools
1981	MISP extended	£30m	IT R&D support
1982	CAD/CAM scheme	£6m	Increase awareness and courses in CAD/CAM
1982–6	Flexible Manufacturing Systems Scheme	£60m	50 per cent grants for consultancy, 33 per cent for development costs
1982–3	Software Product Scheme	£10m	Programme revamped
1983	Software Product Scheme	£25m	Increased funding
1983	Alvey Programme	£200m	50 per cent grants to cooperative IT R&D projects

by the Post Office. The suppliers considered that this equipment would be obsolete within ten years, making such an investment uneconomical. Given that the Post Office was unable to expand its own manufacturing facilities, the government considered increased competition to be a solution to the problem. The break-up of the suppliers' cartel led in time to the development of different technological systems, which was to cause the Post Office massive additional maintenance and integration costs.

In 1965 a Review Committee, set up under Professor Charles Carter, recommended that the Post Office's monopoly on the maintenance and installation of apparatus attached to the telephone network should be withdrawn. The American strategy by which, from 1969 onwards, subscribers had had the option of connecting their own apparatus to the network was held up as an example for the British to emulate. This further increased the pressure for liberalization. British Telecom's manufacturers also supported liberalization, since they felt that their confinement to Post Office specifications was making them uncompetitive.

In 1969 the Post Office allowed the GLC to install an Ericsson exchange, and this was shortly followed by the entry of IBM into the market, with the introduction of a new private exchange geared to both 'voice and data' switching. IBM's product, which was technologically ahead of anything British manufacturers could offer, had considerable customer appeal, and by 1981 IBM had become the market leader in British private exchanges. British manufacturers were at this time working on the development of System X, a prototype version of which was completed in 1979. This came under heavy criticism from the computer community, which argued that it was out of date, too expensive to win export orders, and reflected a lack of computer expertise on the part of the manufacturers. Despite this, BT installed the first System X exchange in 1980, and civil servants remained optimistic about its export potential.

Given the *de facto* entry of foreign firms, and the liberalization of the monopoly in their favour, it was only to be expected that British manufacturers would campaign for legal liberalization, to free them from Post Office specifications.

In 1981, following the election of the Conservative government in 1979, came the Telecommunications Act, which, on the one hand, arranged for BT to be formally separated from the Post

Office, thereby promoting rivalry and competition between the two businesses in borderline areas, e.g. electronic mail, and, on the other hand, made provision for the liberalization of attachments, subject to equipment being of approved standard, with BT retaining its monopoly over the installation of the first instrument. However, the anticipated benefits of the Act were slow to materialize, for two reasons. Firstly, there were considerable delays in the approval of equipment, since BT understandably had little incentive to speed up the procedure for licensing rivals. Secondly, manufacturers supplying BT were reluctant to compete too strongly for fear of losing their orders from BT for the first instrument. No reasonable justification or explanation for the first instrument monopoly was ever given, and it was later abolished. The privatization of BT was finally completed in 1985, although the government, through its 51 per cent share holding, retained significant control.

By stark contrast to the incoherent British policy towards computer and telecommunication companies, those of the Japanese government were a model of consistent order. Between 1962 and 1966 MITI launched Japan's first computer development project, which was immediately followed in 1966–71 by a second. In 1968, having substantial funds at its disposal, Nippon Telephone and Telegraph (NTT) was able to launch its own computer project, in conjunction with NEC, Hitachi and Fijitsu. The principal objective behind the Japanese government's policy, which was reinforced after the oil shocks of the 1970s, was to undermine the dominance of IBM, and to capture for Japan the lion's share of the global IT market. (For a summary of the government's support for the Japanese IT industry see Table 3.)

In 1971 MITI unsuccessfully attempted to restructure the Japanese computer industry by persuading the six major companies to form three pairs for the purposes of research, and in the same year launched a new Pattern Information Processing Project. In addition, throughout the 1970s the government made substantial investment in VLSI (Very Large Scale Integration for Microchips) technology, and facilitated the rapid transfer of technology from government laboratories to industry. Furthermore, in 1976 NTT established the Japan Communication Technology Company, and in 1981 the Japanese Electronics Company, both of

Table 3 Public policy towards information technology in Japan

Year(s)	Title	Value	Notes
1962–6	High Capacity Computer Development Project	Y3.5bn	MITI computer project to help Fujitsu
1966–71	Super High Performance Computer System	Y10bn $97m	MITI computer proproject to help Fujitsu, Hitachi and NEC
1970–82	IT Promotion Agency (IPA)	$70m	Grant to offset agency's expenses
1970–82	Loans for software development	$450m	Provided through IPA
1971–81	Pattern Information Processing (PIPS)	$97m	MITI-funded project
1972–80	Computer peripherals	$290m	MITI programme to develop printers, etc.
1976–9	VLSI Project	$170m	Collaborative R&D project with 100 per cent MITI funding
1977–83	Complex Laser System	Y13bn	
1978–83	Fourth Generation Computer system	$74m	MITI R&D grants
1979–86	Optical Measuring and control system	Y18bn	
1981–8	High speed computer for scientific use	Y30bn $200m	Development of supercomputer
1981–91	Fifth Generation Computer project	$450m	100 per cent funded by MITI in the first instance

which had the clearly defined objective of promoting technology transfer from NTT's laboratories to small and medium-sized companies.

Throughout the post-war period, until 1975, with the exception of IBM and RCA, both of which had been established in Japan before the war, the Japanese government made substantial use of protectionist measures to shield its growing IT industry from the threat of international competition. When, in 1975, global pressure forced Japan to abandon protectionist measures, rigid standards were introduced as a means of restricting foreign competition and it was not until 1982, once Japanese manufacturers were strategically well-positioned to compete effectively, that NTT finally relaxed these standards and allowed US companies to compete in the telecommunications market.

Throughout the post-war period the governments of the USA, Britain and Japan intervened in their domestic IT markets. Despite this, the British and, to a lesser extent, American governments did not establish a coherent and rigorous strategy, in the sense of clearly defined objectives, together with workable mechanisms for achieving them before intervening. The American government, although having no clearly defined policy, did execute a series of decisions that had the effect of reinforcing each other and producing a recognizable IT strategy. Britain, on the other hand, was completely starved of any consistent IT policy, the only uniform feature being the repeated use of telecommunications revenues to subsidize the postal service. While the British government, between 1968 and 1981, did operate a policy of supporting ICL, the decision not to make ICL IBM-compatible meant that its expansion was restricted to the domestic market. The Japanese, by contrast, did adopt an organized, planned approach, which defined goals and regularly assessed their attainability.

Although coherent government policies can be important influences in determining the success of an industry, they are by no means the only factors. The tremendous growth of the US economy, coupled with its status as the world's largest single market, undoubtedly aided the success of American companies, in that it enabled them to establish a firm domestic base from which to launch their attack on the global IT market. Similarly, the Japanese were able to reap the advantages of a large domestic market, which for many years was protected from imports, and hence overseas competition. Britain, however, did not benefit from a large internal market and, despite being a member of the EEC from 1973, was unable to reap similar advantages from the fragmented European market.

Market size was not the only contributory factor. IT is a highly knowledge-based industry, and whilst Britain was responsible for many early inventions in the electronics field, it confined its higher education to a much smaller proportion of the population throughout the post-war period than was the case in America and Japan.

Consequently, Britain produced far fewer adequately qualified personnel, capable of applying high technology to business. Technology transfer is most successful when a company directly recruits competent university students. But even with the growth of the university sector in the 1960s, Britain was still producing far fewer engineers per capita than the USA, Japan, France and Germany, and thereby directly hindering her chances of success in the high technology field.

A further related factor is the high status of academic life in Britain compared with the low status (in academic eyes) of those who work in industry. While this prejudice was undoubtedly reduced in the late 1970s and early 1980s, its effect has been to minimize valuable contact between graduate scientists and engineers working in industry and their former colleagues and tutors remaining in academic life. This contrasts particularly strongly with the situation in Japan, where industrial research is generally regarded more highly than that in the universities, and where professors keep in contact with former students, exchanging ideas and information, often laying the basis for future research projects.

The following chapters will examine in greater detail government and company IT strategies from the early to mid-1980s. Chapter 2 investigates the rise of the Japanese industry to challenge the hegemony of IBM, and the part played by both the government and companies in encouraging and facilitating that development. The subsequent chapters look at the response of the Americans to this Japanese challenge, followed by the European and British attempts to catch up with the established market leaders. The penultimate chapter describes and evaluates the emergence of global coalitions of survival-seeking European IT companies, and discusses the implications of these strategies for their national governments. The final chapter provides a general discussion and critique of the role of public support for the IT industry.

2 The Japanese Challenge

The economic miracle that transformed Japan into one of the largest, most fiercely competitive economies in the world did not occur until after the Second World War. Faced with the total devastation of their industrial base, the Japanese used American financial aid not only to rebuild but also to transform the structure of their economy. By the mid-1960s and early 1970s, armed with advanced high technology and a loyal battalion of inscrutably efficient workers, Japan came to pose a serious and powerful threat to some of the world's most prestigious economies.

Although by the early 1980s the Japanese strategy of export-led growth, combined with industry concentrated investment (leading to the neglect of public amenities and housing), had won for them global market successes in steel, consumer electronics, shipbuilding, pharmaceuticals and cars, Japan had yet to conquer the supreme power of IBM if she was to dominate the IT field. Nevertheless, the Japanese were by this time strategically well positioned to launch an attack on IBM. As seen in Chapter 1, throughout the post-war period the Japanese government had shown itself to be capable of shrewd, tactical planning; protectionist measures had been introduced to protect the developing domestic microelectronics, computer and telecommunications industries; large-scale finance had been made available to promote industrial R&D; a joint industry association, JEIDA, had been set up to coordinate the activities of individual firms; and a 'buy Japanese' procurement policy had been established. Furthermore, the government had founded a company, JECC, to be responsible for financing the leasing of Japanese computers, and, perhaps more importantly, to be responsible for buying basic computer technology patents from IBM at a royalty rate of 5 per cent. Despite repeated allegations, particularly from Europe, that she was operating at an unfair advantage and enjoying a 'free ride' in the international arena, Japan continued to operate these protectionist policies until 1975, when the first serious moves towards liberalization were made.

The first major attempt to push the Japanese computer industry on to a world competitive footing occurred in 1973, largely in response to the sharp rises in oil prices of the early 1970s. For Japan, a country less than 1 per cent sufficient in oil (and only 15 per cent sufficient in food), these price shocks posed an alarming threat to survival. Under the supervision of MITI, an immediate rethink of the Japanese economy took place, as a result of which IT was singled out as being an industry whose successful development could, on the one hand, promote optimum efficiency in the allocation and consumption of resources, and, on the other hand, provide Japan with a high value-added industry, potentially capable of winning valuable export markets.

MITI's initial attempt to restructure the computer industry in 1971, however, was not particularly fruitful. MITI had hoped that by dividing the six major computer manufacturers, for the purposes of R&D, into three pairs – Hitachi–Fujitsu, NEC–Toshiba and Mitsubishi–Oki Electric – and by giving additional assistance through special depreciation allowances, tax concessions, shared development costs, and in some cases export subsidies, mutual cooperation and rapid harmonious development would be promoted. Although the Hitachi–Fujitsu combination was persuaded to produce large IBM–compatible mainframes and Mitsubishi–Oki Electric smaller IBM-compatible computers, the NEC–Toshiba combination was left to design its own, competition between the six rivals remained intense.

By making four out of six of Japan's computer manufacturers compatible with IBM, the government in effect focused attention upon challenging IBM. It forced these companies continually to forecast IBM's development and marketing strategies, in order that rival products could be launched in sufficient time to take a sizeable share of the market. For this policy to be successful, a continuous and reliable flow of information about IBM's plans was required. Consequently, professional IBM-watchers were soon commanding large financial remunerations, in exchange for their future projections and analyses of IBM's policies.

IBM responded to this Japanese challenge by shortening product life cycles and speeding up the volume of shipments. This combined policy brought great pressure to bear on the Japanese companies, driving some of them beyond the limits of the law. In

1982 a number of Hitachi and Mitsubishi employees were charged by the US Department of Justice with engaging in a conspiracy to steal IBM's computer designs and technology, particularly those relating to the M3081 large-scale computer and the M3380 high performance disk subsystem. The companies concerned believed that if they could obtain this information prior to, or concurrent with, IBM's first customer shipment of the new product, this would greatly enhance their ability to respond effectively and capture significant market share.

Given the technical sophistication of these IBM plug compatible Japanese companies, together with their full menu of computer products, it was not long before IBM realized that it was facing a serious challenge to its dominant market position, and, consequently, sought to maintain the secrecy of its systems interconnect architecture (SNA), which was the key to establishing compatibility between its products. In the mid-1980s the European Commission put pressure on IBM to release interface information at the time of product announcement rather than at the time of first shipment (approximately one year later). However, whilst IBM was prepared to reveal this information within six months, it refused to succumb to the Commission's request in full, since by so doing it would have severely endangered its remaining competitive advantage over the Japanese. IBM further argued that providing the Japanese with too much proprietary information would serve to encourage imitation at the expense of innovation.

NEC was one of the two major companies selected by MITI to design its own computers. Free from the constraints of IBM plug compatibility and the pressure of closely following and anticipating IBM's strategies, NEC enjoyed a much greater degree of flexibility than many of its domestic rivals. Furthermore, because of its telecommunications expertise, NEC benefited not only from NTT's custom but also from its generous research budget of $400m in 1983.

NEC first entered the computer market in the 1950s, and in 1962 signed a pact with Honeywell to manufacture (in Japan) computers based on Honeywell designs. By 1985 NEC had taken over this design function from Honeywell, which had begun to sell NEC mainframes in the USA, in addition to using, for some of its series 0 computers, systems control programming developed by NEC.

What the Europeans see?

Source: *Computer Talk*, 6 August 1984.

In 1971, in addition to its attempted reorganization of the computer industry, MITI set up a national research programme, the Pattern Information Processing System Project (PIPS), which ran until 1981, a.:d focused upon the recognition of characters, three-dimensional objects, speech, natural language processing, and such devices as semiconductor lasers. The project also had a significant Artifical Intelligence (AI) component, which was specifically related to Japanese needs and provided a strong foundation for the later Fifth Generation work.

Despite these government initiatives, its dominant position in the domestic market, and a healthy export record (38 per cent of the $5.3 billion output was exported in 1983), the Japanese computer industry continued to experience problems because of limited software developments and the subservient relationship with IBM. Although her hardware was as powerful and competitive as that of the USA, Japan's lag in software meant that the small number of complete systems exported often incorporated mainframes that ran IBM programmes. Many Japanese programmes imitated IBM software, and Fujitsu and Hitachi were forced to make monthly payments amounting to millions of dollars to IBM, to avoid being charged with infringements. Furthermore. because most Japanese can understand English programmes while

Westerners remain mystified by the kanji of Japanese programmes, a one-way trade in software was encouraged. Japan's software development was also hindered by the fact that 90 per cent of
the software used domestically was tailor-made, compared with
only 34 per cent in the US. Japan's most successful software exports
in the late 1970s and 1980s were embedded programmes, often to be
found installed in computerized arcade games.

From the early 1970s MITI attempted to solve these software
problems by encouraging the development of independent software companies, skilled in the art of designing programmes.
However, by 1983 it was still the case that approximately three-
quarters of Japan's software companies were subcontractors to the big
computer manufacturers, following customers' orders rather than
developing and strengthening their independent expertise.

The Japanese realized that if they were going to supplant IBM
and become the world's commanding force in the computer
industry, it was imperative that their software should be greatly
improved, and their particular linguistic difficulties overcome.
Japanese writing normally uses a minimum of 2000 kanji, which is
too many characters for normal computer programmes to
accommodate. As a consequence, programming had been carried
out by means of English words and English versions of Japanese
syllables, which meant that Japanese programmers required,
although they did not receive, more training than their counterparts in the US and Europe. Because of this, in 1978, Matsataka
Nakano, a bureaucrat without scientific training working for the
Electronic Policy Division of MITI, suggested that the MITI
Electrotechnical Laboratory should develop a 'software-less' computer. Although this idea was initially received with scepticism,
the timing of the proposal was particularly opportune, since, on
the one hand, MITI's existing research projects were nearing
completion, and, on the other, MITI was becoming ever increasingly concerned with the software problem.

MITI had originally thought that its strategy of persuading
Fujitsu, Hitachi, Mitsubishi and Oki Electric to manufacture
IBM-compatible computers would guarantee the industry's surviv-
al, saving it from destruction by IBM's world-beating system 370.
However, in reality, this policy had created a severely pressurized
environment for the companies concerned, as they frantically and

desperately attempted to follow developments within IBM. Consequently, at the beginning of 1979, MITI put together an advisory committee, chaired by Professor Tohru Moto-Oka of Tokyo University, and composed mainly of academics, whose functions was, with a budget of $400 000, to devise a research programme that would both free Japanese companies from IBM and provide a solution to the software problem.

The work of this committee, lasting two years and assimilating ideas on a world-wide scale from academics (particularly AI experts) and journals, formed the basis of Japan's Fifth Generation Computer Project. This project had the ambitious goal of building a computer with common sense: a computer remembering 20 000 rules about the real world, and 100 million facts, would, it was hoped, be able to communicate with people through the media of speech and pictures.

In October 1981 MITI sponsored a conference to launch the Fifth Generation Computer Project, and insisted that foreign universities, companies and governments should be invited to cooperate with Japanese institutions in this exciting venture. Whatever the reasons for this display of hospitality, which was seen by many as a cosmetic exercise to reduce trade friction and enhance Japan's image abroad, there were no immediate acceptances. In 1981 the project's members included eight firms (Fujitsu, Hitachi, NEC, Mitsubishi, Oki, Matsushita, Sharp and Toshiba) and two national laboratories (the NTT's Musashino Laboratories, and MITI's own Electrotechnical Laboratory (ETL)). Approximately forty of Japan's brightest engineers, all under the age of 35, were hand-picked from each of the firms and laboratories. They gathered at the new Institute for Fifth Generation Computer Technology (ICOT) in Tokyo in April 1982, and provision was made for the establishment of an informal working committee, which would, for the first time, allow academics, who were usually forbidden to serve outside their university, to contribute directly to the project. (For a list of the members of the FGCS Research and Planning Committee see Table 4.)

The project was led by Kazuhiro Fuchi, who had worked at the ETL for twenty-four years, constantly struggling against policies which he thought constituted barriers to research in Japan. In particular, he felt that ETL's isolation from corporate and uni-

Table 4 Members of the FGCS Research and Planning Committee

Firms	Members	Institutes and Associations	Members	Universities	Members
Fujitsu	7	ETL	15	Tokyo	11
NEC	7	Yokosuka-ECL of the NTT	3	Keio	2
Mitsubishi	6	NTT	2	Kyoto	2
Hitachi	5	Musashino-ECL of the NTT	1	Waseda	1
Toshiba	5	JIPDEC	2	Seikei	1
Oki	4	IPA	1	Tohoku	1
Matsushita	3	JIPA	1	Tokyo Un. of Science	1
Sharp	3	JECC	1	Hokkaido	1
Mitsui Shipbuilding	1	Institute of Future Technology	1	Gasshuin	1
Fuji Bank	1	Japan Software Industry Association	1	Tokyo Institute of Technology	1
Nihon Keizai Shimbun	1				
Total 43		Total 28		Total 22	

versity scientists, its minuscule research budget and rigid research hierarchy, which prevented able young scientists from contributing to advanced projects, produced a stifling, oppressing environment, and he was determined that ICOT should not make the same mistakes.

The ten-year Fifth Generation Project was divided into three stages. The first, three-year, stage, funded entirely by the government and completed in 1984, was devoted to the development of a prototype machine, a personal PROLOG workstation. (A PROLOG workstation is an advanced software tool, which can be used for developing new software systems.) The second, four-year, stage was intended to concentrate upon engineering, experimentation, and prototyping, and was to be responsible for investigations into systems integration and parallel processing. More advanced research investigations into these areas would be conducted in the third and final three-year stage (see Figure 5).

Although all the sub-projects, and the control of finances, were to be strictly supervised by ICOT, it was not the intention that all this work should be executed within ICOT. Hence, it was arranged that each week the ICOT researchers would return to their companies to communicate the progress being made, and provide an opportunity for those firms which were interested to apply for contract work in areas where they considered themselves to already have an advantage or valuable contribution to make.

Despite the fact that national projects in Japan had generally comprised a partnership between government and private funds, the Fifth Generation participants argued that they could not afford to finance such a high risk project, in addition to supporting it by providing teams of top researchers. MITI appreciated this, and subsequently agreed to underwrite the project for the first three years, after which it was hoped that the firms would be able to make financial contributions towards the estimated expenditure of $200m.

ICOT and the Fifth Generation Project did not meet with the approval of all Japanese companies. Besides the general reluctance to invest in what appeared to be a very risky and highly speculative scheme, and annoyance at being unable to dictate the research agenda to ICOT, many companies resented having to sacrifice prime researchers to work alongside competitors, since

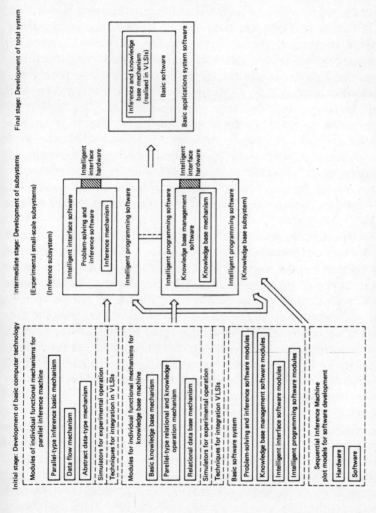

Figure 5 Stages of Fifth Generation Computer R&D
Source: ICOT, *Outline of Fifth Generation Computer Project*, 1984.

they feared that this might erode loyalty to the company. In addition, there were those who considered ICOT's goals to be over-ambitious, as Hiroshi Yamoda, Director of Fujitsu's Laboratories explained to *Fortune* in October 1982: 'ICOT's work may trigger some commercial systems, but from a business standpoint we're not sure that we can make a computer with a human brain.'

MITI considered that the development of Fifth Generation computers would enable Japan to deal successfully with its ageing society and the incumbent problems of medical and welfare care, to provide the physically handicapped with the opportunity to lead more active and fulfilled lives, and through the propagation of distribution systems, enhance the quality of life by enabling greater numbers of people to work at home. MITI was also confident that a successful Fifth Generation programme would, at the domestic level, lead to maximum efficiency in the consumption of resources, by providing the perfect solution to the peak-load problem, and internationally give Japan the competitive edge over IBM.

Recognizing the ability of Japan's computer industry to exploit the fruits of advanced research, and to secure distribution channels throughout Europe and the USA for its expertly marketed products, many Western observers feared that Japan's Fifth Generation Project might, from their point of view, prove to be disastrously successful. Although by the end of its ten-year life the project was expected, and indeed seemed likely, to make several IT break-throughs, it was equally clear that the short run would provide the opportunity to exploit the commercial potential of specific developments, in particular the speech-driven word processor and the English–Japanese translator.

Indeed, shortly after commencement, companies taking part in the project were busily investigating the possibility of applying the latest developments in speech and vision recognition to calculators, videos, television sets and electronic games. This led many of ICOT's more suspicious critics, especially in British industry and government, to suggest that the Japanese had deceived the world into providing scientists for a project which, behind the grandiose, publicly stated goals, was basically designed to promote the continued expansion of Japan's consumer electronics industry. Further suspicions were aroused when, on arriving in Tokyo to discuss the possibility of joint ventures, members of the Alvey Directorate were informed that ICOT would be willing to cooperate only with British universities, not British companies. This strongly suggested to Brian Oakley that the Japanese were trying to get something for nothing out of Britain.

Despite these suspicions, in November 1984 ICOT demonstrated its PROLOG workstation, which heralded the successful completion of the first three-year phase of the Fifth Generation Project. This was shortly followed by the development of the first Japanese-to-English machine translation system, by Hitachi, Fujitsu and Bravice International, and although by 1985 IBM (Japan) had produced a similar machine, Fujitsu's Atlas II system was by far the most powerful. This was interpreted by some as evidence that Japan had beaten IBM and become the world's AI leader, a claim that seemed to be further sustained when in 1984–85 both IBM and DEC established new research laboratories in Japan.

We have seen how Japan's decision to concentrate upon establishing supremacy in the field of IT, together with MITI's encouragement in the 1970s of moves towards IBM-compatibility, led to intense competition, not only with IBM but also with other American and European computer companies. By the beginning of the 1980s a fierce battle was raging for IT market shares, and the Japanese realized that they could no longer afford to be even one small step behind IBM. The merging of computing and telecommunications at this time, and the need it created for a major reappraisal within the IT industry, were considered by Japan to provide her with the opportunity she needed to conquer America in general, and IBM in particular. Because Japan reacted immediately to this challenge, she gained a tenuous but uncertain advantage over America.

In the chapters that follow we shall examine the reactions of America and Europe to this vigorous new challenge. Whilst the Japanese goals were fairly clearly specified, the means by which they hoped to reach them was far from apparent to the outside world. Furthermore, American and European observers expressed considerable confusion over the relation which existed, if any, between the Fifth Generation Computer project and other non-computing aspects of the Japanese electronics industry. As a consequence, the first and most crucial hurdle facing America and

Europe was to assess what the Japanese challenge amounted to, since only then could an appropriate plan of action be drawn up. America was the first to respond, and accordingly it is to an examination of its response that we now turn.

3 The American Response

By the beginning of the 1980s America had become increasingly concerned about the threat of Japanese competition; electronics companies in particular were calling for government intervention to curb what they considered to be an excessive level of Japanese imports. The Japanese strategy of targeting particular market segments, and then using their highly developed manufacturing techniques and marketing skills to produce and distribute high-quality low-cost products, had already won them the lion's share of the world consumer electronics market (televisions, stereos, calculators, electronic toys and digital watches), and was beginning to threaten the US semiconductor industry.

By the end of 1982 the Japanese had taken over the market for memory devices, and accounted for 70 per cent of the supply of all 64K RAMs. This development was viewed with considerable alarm by US semiconductor companies, which feared that without experience of building 64K RAMs they might not be able to maintain the technology lead which they had developed in the production of other devices, including micro-processors. Furthermore, they realized that unless successful strategies to combat Japanese dominance were quickly formulated, Japan would rapidly emerge as the market leader of the next generations of memory devices – the 128K and 256K RAMs.

Faced with this threat, American companies began to collaborate in joint ventures designed to spread the enormous costs of product development. One member of the Semiconductor Industry Association explained: 'As technology moved forward, companies came to the conclusion that they, by themselves, couldn't afford the costs of keeping up.' The most significant of these early collaborations were the agreement between Advanced Micro Devices and Intel, and the establishment of an industry-supported Semiconductor Research Cooperative (SRC), aimed at financing long-term research in US universities.

The SRC, born out of the worry and concern of members of the Semiconductor Industry Association, was set up in the Research Triangle Park in North Carolina in September 1982, with thirty members, including IBM, Advanced Micro Devices, Control Data, Digital Equipment, Honeywell, Monolithic Memories, National Semiconductor and Silicon Systems (for a full list, see Table 5). Its major objective was to prevent the US semiconductor industry from disappearing, by increasing the number of high quality engineering graduates, and by advancing research in the electronics field. The SRC, with a total budget of $12m, set about funding fifty-three projects in thirty-five US universities in three main areas: microstructure, design, and manufacturing science (see Table 6).

Whilst US computer manufacturers, including IBM, may have been concerned about the Japanese threat to the US semiconductor industry, this did not prevent them from taking advantage of the low prices offered by Japanese suppliers. In 1981, before the establishment of the SRC, Hewlett-Packard had published chip expenditure information, detailing specifications and requirements of 64K RAMs, and had explained that until a US company was able to produce high-quality low-cost chips comparable with Japan, it would continue to take advantage of Japanese suppliers. Furthermore, US semiconductor companies themselves found that

Table 5   SRC membership (April 1984)

Advanced Micro Devices Inc.	LSI Logic
Burroughs	Monolithic Memories Inc.
Control Data Corporation	Monsanto
Digital Equipment Corporation	Motorola Inc.
DuPont	National Semiconductor
Eaton	Corporation
E Systems	Perkin-Elmer Corporation
General Electric	RCA
General Instrument Corporation	Rockwell
Goodyear Aerospace	SEMI-CHAPTER
Harris	Silicon Systems Inc.
Hewlett Packard Company	Union Carbide Corporation
Honeywell Inc.	Vanan
IBM Corporation	Westinghouse Electric Corporation
Intel Corporation	Xerox

Table 6   SRC Centres of Excellence and Programme Centres

Cornell University	SRC Center for Microstructure and Technology
University of California at Berkeley	Design Center for CAD/IC
Carnegie-Mellon University	SRC/Carnegie-Mellon University Design Automation/Computer Aided Design Center
Renssalaer Polytechnic Institute	Advanced Beam Systems Technology Program
MIT	Three-dimensional circuits and systems technology program
University of California, Santa Barbara	Program in Gallium Arsenide digital device technology
University of Michigan	Program for automation in semi-conductor manufacturing
Stanford University	Program on manufacturing science and technology

buying competitively priced Japanese parts to make systems products made economic sense.

However, for the US computer industry, this dependence upon a competitor, Japan, for supplies of 64K RAMs was regarded as highly unsatisfactory. If the Japanese decided to restrict or terminate supplies, this could have disastrous consequences.

The Japanese computer challenge began at the bottom end of the market, with low cost personal computers, threatening in particular Tandy and Apple, in the early 1980s. However, by this date many American producers were already using parts supplied by Japanese manufacturers. Especially in computer peripherals, 'Made in Japan' began to appear on an ever increasing percentage of printers, keyboards, video terminals and other add-on equipment. Even IBM, once the leader in printer technology, began buying printers from Japan.

Although by 1981 the big US computer manufacturers had yet to be challenged by the Japanese, IBM, in spite of dominating the US and European markets, had been ousted as the leading supplier of computers in the Japanese market. Some Japanese-

Table 7   Joint ventures, joint agreements, and technical exchanges

Companies	Manufacturing/ terminals	Networks	Marketing services
IBM/Nippon	Fax Termninals		
Scientific		Cable satellite	
Actanta			
Plessey			
Zenith/Taft			Teletext
Burroughs/Intel	IC chips		
Xerox/Intel/DEC		Local area network	
Xerox/Intel/DEC		Local area network	
AT&T/CBS			Videotext
Fujitsu/TRW	IC chips		
Texas Instru- ments/IBM		Local area network	
Microdyne/ Domesticom		Master satellite antenna systems	
New York Times/ CBS			Videotext
Western Union/ Airfone			Air telephone service Cellular radio
Northern Telecom/ GE			
OAK/RACAL		Pay TV/Satellite	
GEC/Marconi/ Nippon Ericsson/ Anaconda	Telephone systems		
Timex/Sinclair	Personal computers		
American Satellite Continental Tele- phone			
GCA/Matra	Semiconductor equipment		
Intel/NEC	Microprocessors		
Motorola/NEC	Pocket pagers		
AT&T/GTE			Cellular radio
AT&T/N.V. Philips		Digital switch	
Sperry/Mitsu- bishi	Office automation		

Table 7 contd.

Companies	Manufacturing/ terminals	Networks	Marketing services
Siemens/Western /Digital	IC chips		
Columbia/HBO/ CBS			Movie software
AT&T/Plessey			Cellular radio
Com Sat/IBM/ Aetna		Satellite net	
Alcatel/N.V. Philips	Recording drives	Cellular radio switches	
IBM/Kanematsu-Gaslto			Electronic typewriter
Control Data/N.V. Philips			
GTE/Italtel		Central office switches	
American Express/ Warner Com-munications			Videotext

Source: 'IBM and Intel Link Up to Fend off Japan', *Business Week*, 10 January 1983: and 'Giants Enter Ventures as Partners in Prosperity', *Electronic Business*, January 1983.

built mainframe computers were, by this time, on sale in the US, but under the name of National Advanced Systems, a company selling Hitachi built IBM-compatible computers in addition to its own. Another American company, TRW, went one step further and formed a joint venture company with Fujitsu, to market Japanese computers in the US. As production techniques advanced, and the pace of innovation increased, many American companies began to realize that the only way to survive in this fiercely competitive, rapidly changing market was to form partnerships and develop inter-company divisions of labour (see Table 7). NCR, which had at one time made every part of the computers it sold, began working with outsiders, including Convergent Technologies, Intel and Ztel. This trend towards collaboration became increasingly important to the industry, and, as a consequence, in an attempt to cement newly formed relationships many

Table 8   Information-processing companies buy into one another

Investor	Company invested in	Size of investment (millions of dollars)	Equity position (per cent)
Control Data	Centronics	$25	35
Control Data	Source Telecomputing	5	30–40
IBM	Intel	250	12
IBM	Rolm	228	15
NCR	Ztel	NA	19
Sperry	Trilogy	42	15
Sperry	Magnetic Peripherals	40 *	13
Western Union	Vitalink	11.5	25

*Estimate.
NA = not available.

Source: *Business Week*, 11 July 1983.

companies began to invest in their partners. Table 8 lists a number of American companies that had invested in each other by July 1983.

NCR and Sperry both invested in a technical partner in 1983, and IBM legitimized the trend by buying 12 per cent of Intel and 15 per cent of Rolm. It was said that 'not even IBM could invest enough research money to have every widget necessary to compete today'.

Threatened with the reality of losing ever-increasing market shares to the Japanese, the US computing industry, to a certain extent, followed the initiative of the semiconductor industry, and began to discuss seriously the potential of collaborative R&D. Williams Norris of Control Data Corporation arranged a meeting, in Orlando, Florida, in February 1982 between senior executives from fifteen computer companies and two trade associations, a representative of the Massachusetts Institute of Technology (MIT), and the Under Secretary of Denfence, Richard De Lauer, who was also the Pentagon's R&D Director. This assembly arranged to do two things: firstly, to create the Microelectronics and Computer Technology Corporation (MCC), and, secondly, to put together task teams to define areas of research which should be undertaken. Norris told *Electronics* (10 March 1982) that the MCC had been set up to counter 'A government-led effort by Japan to replace the US as world leader in computers and microelectronics.'

Both the MCC, and any research projects it recommended were to be limited to US-based companies, and initially, although this was later modified, there were to be no public sector participants. To comply with anti-trust regulations it was necessary for the MCC to seek clearance from the Federal Trade Commission. Despite Norris's confidence, this clearance was not granted as readily as had been expected, and although by December 1982 the Justice Department had announced that it had no objections to the formation of the MCC, legislation still had to be passed by Congress, providing anti-trust exemption for proposed (and actual) joint R&D ventures.

One of the fundamental objectives of the MCC was to reduce, if not eliminate, the enormous duplication of effort by individual computer and microelectronic companies, thereby promoting greater efficiency in the utilization of investment captial, and providing a partial, short-term solution to the problems arising from shortages of trained scientific and engineering personnel.

Although the initial reaction of the executives attending the Orlando meeting (February 1982) was largely positive, there were those who expressed certain fundamental reservations. Many recognized that persuading competing companies to engage in collaborative R&D projects would not be an easy task, since it would require a substantial change in traditional American management attitudes. Texas Instruments' Assistant Vice-President for Strategic Planning, Charles H. Phipp, said that it was 'probably unlikely that we would become a participant' and felt that the MCC was 'certainly foreign to our past experience'. Mostek's Harold L. Ergpolt Jr requested further information before deciding whether or not to join, and admitted to *Electronics* (10 March 1982): 'I just don't know if I'm ready to move with competitors against a common objective.' However, the two trade association presidents, Peter McCloskey of the Electrical Industries Association and Vizo E. Henrigner of the Computer and Business Equipment Manufacturers Association, were both optimistic about the future of the MCC.

In the event it took two years to get the MCC established. Gerry Ginneer, Vice-President for Science and Technology at Honeywell, recalled to *Datamation* (15 May 1984), 'It took a lot of talking to convince a number of people that the challenges we all faced were great enough that we had to make some adjustments', and added, 'Companies had to be willing to share technology in some areas where they felt they had invested a lot of money and attained some strength. That was why the formation of MCC took a while'.

The MCC also represented a marked divergence from the previous pattern of cooperative ventures, such as the SRC. Unlike the SRC, which collected money and then distributed it between colleges and universities, the MCC undertook to do its own research.

The MCC held its first board meeting in Austin, Texas, in February 1983, to discuss four projects and a broad set of goals, which had been compiled by the task teams. (For a list of MCC members see Table 9.) The shortest of these, the integrated circuits project, was designed to last six years; the software technology project seven years; and the computer-aided design and computer-aided manufacturing project, which had nine of the thirteen companies investing in it, was designed to last eight years. Finally, the advanced computer design project was expected to take ten years to complete. It was the task teams' belief that technological break-throughs had to be made in these four basic areas before the MCC could finalize its long-term programme.

The decision to locate the MCC at Austin, Texas, had been largely financial. Generous private sector assistance had been promised; and, in addition, considerable state, local government and university support had been shown for the project. Hence, by locating at Austin, Texas, the MCC would have immediate access to substantial funds, thereby avoiding the lengthy, often costly delays caused by the slow acting bureaucracy of the state legislature. It was further felt that Austin, Texas, could provide the necessary research-conducive environment, since there was already a large amount of private investment in the universities, major investment in equipment, a plan to create thirty additional professorships between 1983 and 1986 and $750 000 a year available in grant aid for computer science graduates.

Table 9   MCC members (October 1984)

Advanced Micro Devices
Allied
BMG Industries
Control Data Corporation
Digital Equipment Corporation
Kodak
Gould
Harris
Honeywell
Lockheed
Martin Marietta
Mostek
Motorola
National Semiconductor
NCR
RCA
Rockwell
Sperry

Source: *Computing*, 11 October 1984.

For each MCC project in which they invested, companies were allowed to nominate certain of their scientists, who would return once the research was complete, and a liaison officer. Although normal investment practice, the organizers of the MCC were nonetheless disappointed that participating companies were only prepared to commit themselves to three years' funding.

In January 1983 Admiral Bobby Ray Inman was appointed President of the MCC, bringing with him considerable experience of handling government departments. He had retired from the navy in July 1982, after a long career, with appointments at almost every US intelligence organization, including that of Head of the National Security Agency. It was hoped that Admiral Inman's expertise would prove to be an invaluable asset, since, although the MCC had not originally aimed at seeking government sponsorship, there was a growing conviction among members that circumstances could arise in which links with the government would prove to be beneficial. Inman explained to the *Communication of the ACM* (September 1983) that:

> As long as the government protect our proprietary data, we will make our research very visible to the various government departments. If they see an area where they think there is a national security application, and they want to accelerate or broaden our research, we will discuss with them the ways that this could be done.

Given its private orientation, the MCC was anxious to protect technology developments until they could be exploited by the investing companies. However, since not all shareholders had invested in every project, the MCC faced a further complication in that it would be necessary to protect the interests of those who had invested in a particular project against those who had not. Consequently, it was arranged that where such an exchange was considered to be mutually beneficial, scientists from different companies working on different projects would be permitted to discuss information concerning distinct approaches to solving basic problems. However, where research led to actual application and product development, those companies which had invested in the project were to be allowed three years, after which the MCC would licence this technology to the other participating companies. Hence, within the MCC, because of the necessity for protecting vested interests, the extent to which there could be genuine cooperation and dissemination of ideas was strictly limited.

The MCC was regarded by many as the 'Bunch's' response to the Japanese threat. (The 'Bunch' is a term used to denote all American mainframe and minicomputer manufacturers bar IBM, i.e. 'the rest'.) IBM was not included within this consortium, which was not surprising, given its determination to keep its R&D programme as secret as possible. In spite of this, IBM did recognize that the trend towards university and industry collaboration could be potentially very fruitful. Accordingly, in 1983, it announced that it was making a $50m grant of computer systems to universities, and it began searching the universities of the world, with particular success in Sweden and Australia, for research teams and individual researchers who would be willing to work for the company either on a full-time or part-time basis at the Yorktown Heights Research Headquarters. However, those researchers selected from the Israeli Weizman Institute were allowed to remain on site, despite becoming full-time IBM employees.

This strategy was soon to be imitated by a number of other large American computer giants. In particular, Hewlett-Packard founded a Research Fellowship in software engineering at Oxford University, and set up a research centre near Bristol in England, partly to coordinate its 'consultants' working within UK universities, but also to act as a head-hunting arm, offering large salaries and excellent facilities to disillusioned and underpaid British academics. The success of these American policies resulted in many computer science departments in Britain becoming increasingly concerned about their ability to survive, and in particular to retain their most able researchers. Henry Thomas, of Edinburgh University, undertook consultancy work, much of which was for Plessey, which ensured that he received an attractive financial package. As a result, the Edinburgh department was confident that it could survive at least until 1988 (when the Alvey programme came up for renewal). However, at Imperial College, London the following sentiment was expressed: 'The national strategy is in fact conning people in British universities to work very hard for very little.'

This American recruitment policy was viewed with considerable alarm by the UK government, especially when John Taylor, who had been responsible for compiling the Alvey IKBS study, eventually succumbed to a highly paid job within Hewlett-Packard.

The policy of donating computer systems to universities, thereby acquiring valuable and reliable information about the computer's performance, was not confined to IBM; it was in fact a strategy exploited by many American computer companies, including Xerox, which provided Professor Roger Needham's Computing Laboratory in Cambridge University with a complete Xerox system. Recognizing the increasing difficulties being faced by British computer science departments, some of the large UK electronics companies decided to provide universities with some of the resources that were so desperately required. For example, ICL

Source: *New Scientist*, 1 December 1983.

donated funds for research assistants at Imperial College, London, and GEC provided considerable financial support for Professor Tony Hoare's department at Oxford. However, compared with the scale of US assistance, the funds were meagre.

In addition to these private programmes and strategies, throughout the 1980s, the US government was also sponsoring a number of initiatives designed to promote the American microelectronics industry. These included the Very High Speed Integrated Circuit (VHSIC) programme, the DoD's Software Technology for Adaptable and Reliable Systems (STARS) programme, and the Defence Advanced Research Projects Agency (DARPA) Strategic Computing Programme, for which $600m had been allocated for its first five years. The DARPA project aimed at exploiting promising advances in microelectronics, computer concepts and artificial intelligence. In addition, it was also designed to stimulate broad corporate and university research through research contracts. One of the project's goals was a robot vehicle able to navigate autonomously over roads and through woods at 35 mph, guided by artificial vision and other senses.

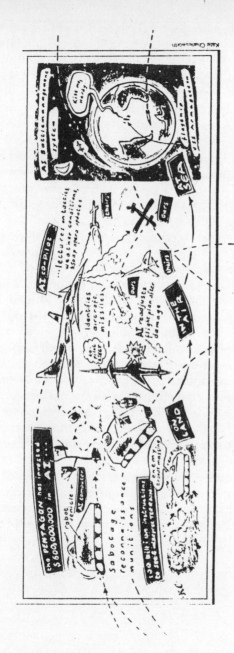

DARPA's AI investment

Source: New Scientist, 15 November 1984

This chapter has revealed the seriousness with which the Americans viewed the Japanese challenge, and has attempted to describe and explain the American response. In addition to establishing a rival Fifth Generation Project, and joint research initiatives, American companies through collaboration and financial partnerships prepared themselves to meet the Japanese attack, and to reap the later benefits of industrial colaboration. In particular, firms soon learnt that by forming coalitions of experts and specialists from different branches of IT, it would be possible to present the customer with a highly competitive package.

The response of the US government was less immediate than that of the threatened companies. Although Congress did remove the anti-trust restrictions on R&D cooperatives, and gave them some tax breaks, the government provided the industry with little direct aid. In an attempt to maintain, if not sharpen, America's competitive computing edge, the Department of Defence developed a series of programmes aimed at 'pulling through' new products via procurement (most notably in the form of the STARS project). The government also provided limited infrastructural support through the establishment of new or additional positions in IT subjects in universities, and by purchasing new super computers for a series of carefully selected universities. Hence, whereas American companies actively responded to the Japanese threat, with former arch rivals burying the hatchet and cooperating, particularly in R&D, the US government assumed a more passive role, relying on procurement and infrastructural support.

In the next chapters we examine the European response to the Japanese initiative, first at the level of the EEC, and then within Britain in particular. Whereas at the beginning of the 1980s America was pre-eminent in computing, and well placed to fight off the Japanese attack, the Europeans had slipped to the position of a poor third, and were ill-prepared to meet this new wave of competition.

4 The European Response

Although by the 1980s Europe constituted approximately one-third of the world market for electronics, European manufacturers were in a weak position, supplying only 10 per cent of the world and 40 per cent of domestic IT markets. In 1975 the European Community had enjoyed a trade surplus in IT of 1.7 billion ECU; by 1984 this surplus had been turned into a 5 billion ECU deficit. By 1981 the Japanese had completed their VLSI project, and were on the threshold of their Fifth Generation Computer initiative; while IBM, as a consequence of large-scale, innovative and highly successful research, commanded 50 per cent of the European computer market. By contrast, the position of European manufacturers, which were estimated to be devoting 80 per cent of their R&D expenditure to catching up, appeared to be far less secure.

The European industry was widely felt to be backward in IT technology. This backwardness was attributed to a number of factors. Some felt that it was the companies which were at fault. Derek Roberts of GEC commented that:

> The balance of payments situation we find ourselves with today really reflects the way industry behaved ten or twenty years ago, because if I go back ten or twenty years, I do not feel in those days we paid enough attention, as we do or have done more recently, to world markets, world competition and world opportunities. (*House of Lords: Session 1984–85, 8th Report, Select Committee on the European Communities: ESPRIT, with Minutes of Evidence.*)

Others felt that disparities in public support for IT between countries had played a major part in disadvantaging European companies. Many within the European Commission and industry felt that the scale of US government support for the American electronics industry meant that non-US producers could not hope to compete effectively, unless they secured comparable financial backing. Viscount Davignon, the Commissioner for Industry, was particularly persuaded by this argument. Consequently, the Commission, along with leading European industrialists, began in the early 1980s to structure a European support programme which, it was hoped, would rectify this imbalance.

Two highly successful models for developing high technology industries existed for the Europeans to follow. First, there was the American procurement–competitive approach, founded on massive government support, combined with substantial venture capital to encourage private sector developments. Second, there stood the Japanese protectionism–collaboration model, which allowed Japanese companies to build, through domestic competition, a firm industrial base, before attacking world markets. In the event, however, neither of these models was directly adopted by the Commission.

Throughout the period 1960–80 individual member states of the European Community pursued national procurement policies aimed at supporting national champions; but these were too small relative to the US to create powerful companies. This national champion policy also had the effect of disintegrating the European market, by means of technical barriers (in the form of different national market standards), and trade barriers (in the form of tariffs). On the research side, national programmes were aimed at supporting domestic manufacturers, e.g. Siemens in West Germany, ICL in the UK, and STET in Italy; while, in the sphere of telecommunications, separate national monopoly administrations developed their own distinctive technologies: buying from domestic firms and implementing their own tariff and service policies, which further reduced the possibility of large-scale, low-cost transnational business services characteristic of the USA.

Although it was not until the beginning of the 1980s that, largely owing to the indefatigable efforts of Viscount Davignon, any serious developments towards European cooperation were to be seen, throughout the 1970s Chris Layton, the Commission's Director responsible for the Electronics sector, repeatedly attempted to initiate Community action; and, in 1974, the Brandt–Heath–Pompidou summit identified several areas, ranging from technology development to the protection of the environment, which provided ample scope for a coordinated policy of European cooperation. However, from the modest beginnings of a small-scale microelectronics and data-processing applications programme adopted in 1979, a Community data-processing policy was developed, and that gave rise to some interesting spin-offs, including STELLA, a joint project for high speed data transmission, and CADDIA, which was a feasibility study into the application of information relating to Community imports, exports and agricultural markets.

With the onset of the 1980s, realizing that major markets such as the consumer electronics market were rapidly being lost to Japan and the USA, Europe began seriously to consider the question of collaboration. Viscount Davignon encouraged twelve of Europe's leading electronics companies to form a Round Table, to discuss the possibility of joint European industrial strategies (The twelve companies were ICL, GEC, Plessey, AEG, Siemens, Nixdorf, Thomson CSF, CII Honeywell Bull, Compagnie Générale de L'Electricé, Philips, Olivetti, and STET.) At the same time, many of the national champions in Europe were becoming increasingly aware of the fact that, even with the protection given by public procurement policies, the size of their domestic markets was not sufficient to ensure them future growth, or to preserve them in the face of every-increasing global competition.

The European Commission was keen to form a relationship with these worried companies, and in 1982 asked the twelve participants of the Round Table to form a Steering Committee, entrusted with the task of studying the feasibility of European collaborative effort, in R&D, defining the level of public support required from the Community, and encouraging the spirit of collaboration in the five priority areas of computer-aided design, microelectronics, software, man–machine interface, and information dissemination.

The Commission was especially concerned with the health of the European electronics industry. By the beginning of the 1980s the collapse of the European consumer electronics industry looked almost a foregone conclusion. While Viscount Davingnon felt that European companies would have the greatest difficulty in remaining competitive with the market leaders in consumer electronics, he nevertheless felt that they should not be prepared to sit back and relinquish the whole of this area to the Japanese, since by so doing they would severely jeopardize their chances of success in other fields, such as IT. In Davignon's words:

You cannot give the Japanese the video recorder market and imagine that with the benefits from that they are not going to do things with it ... If we make the mistake of not creating the conditions to be a competitive producer of many products we are going to make it much more difficult for these companies to keep abreast of change and make it much more difficult for the economies of the various states to channel support money which should go to the industries which have to adapt.

The European Strategic Programme of Research and Development in Information Technology (ESPRIT) was born from discussions between Davignon and the twelve. Its aim was to provide Europe with an internationally competitive IT base, by encouraging collaborative research between European firms, universities and other research bodies. Mike Watson, Technical Director of ICL commented: 'Our understanding of ESPRIT and our only reason for participation is to build a European based force in the economic battles of the next few decades.'

From the Commission's point of view, this objective could be met by fulfilling three goals. The first was to promote industrial cooperation at the pre-competitive stage, the second was to provide the technology base needed to be competitive in the IT market by the end of the 1980s and 1990s, and the third was to pave the way towards European standards for the IT industry. In Luxembourg on 30 June 1982 a Council meeting of Research Ministers affirmed the urgent need for action in the field of collaborative IT R&D; and on 21 December 1982 the Council approved the Commission proposal for a pilot phase of projects, to begin in 1983, and designed to last one year, which would begin to develop the complex machinery necessary for the management of ESPRIT. The subsequent rapid call for pilot project applicants received an extremely favourable response from over 200 companies and universities, in the light of which thirty-eight contracts were awarded.

After successful starts to the pilot projects, on 13 December 1983 the Council accepted the Commission's proposals for a full ESPRIT programme, although the British continued to disagree over the question of EEC financing of the programme. This disagreement was attributed in public statements to concern about the UK's contributions to the EEC budget; the actual reason was to do with infighting at Whitehall. After lengthy rows between the Treasury (which thought the British contribution to ESPRIT should come from funds already allocated to the DTI), and the DTI (which thought the Treasury should be responsible for funding ESPRIT), the decision to adopt the main ESPRIT programme was finally taken by the Council on 28 February 1984, with British approval. (The Treasury eventually backed down and agreed to provide additional funds for the programme.)

The main programme laid down that the budget for ESPRIT was to be 1500m ECU, (approximately £885m) over five years, half of which was to be provided by the Community, and half by the participants. Responsibility for the day-to-day running of ESPRIT was given to a specially created IT Task Force within the Commission, whose function was to deal with calls for proposals, to handle the evaluation of applications, to place contracts and monitor projects. The IT Task Force was advised by a Management Committee comprising representatives of the member states, whose official duty was to provide for the long-term development of ESPRIT, and to approve major projects requiring more than 5m ECU of Community funds. It was hoped that the Management Committee, by virtue of its composition, would provide an important link between ESPRIT and the national IT R&D programmes. Gradually the Steering Committee formed from the original Round Table of twelve IT companies was superseded by a more broadly based ESPRIT Advisory Board.

From the outset the Commission made clear that ESPRIT did not represent an overall strategic plan for Europe's IT industry. In reality it represented the first step towards encouraging greater European cooperation in basic pre-competitive research.

The first call for ESPRIT proposals was announced immediately after the decision of 28 February 1984. By the time the deadline of 7 May 1984 had passed, 441 separate proposals had been submitted to the Commission. These were given a detailed technical evaluation by independent experts, before a final selection was shortlisted (see Figure 6). Awarding of the first contracts was scheduled for July 1984, but in the event was delayed until

December, because of disagreements over financing arrangements. Finally, ninety proposals were selected for funding, incorporating 25 of the thirty-eight original pilot schemes.

Despite the large number of company submissions made to the Commission, and the close industry connection with the preparation of the programme, many industrialists, both at a general and specific level, expressed reservations about the nature of ESPRIT. Certain critics suggested that by emphasizing research the Community was tackling the wrong issue, and argued that it was not so much a research as a marketing and product development problem that was facing Europe's high technology industries. ICL argued that in some areas, particularly microelectronics, the real gap between Europe and Japan and the USA was not in the underlying technology but in production and marketing. At a conference in

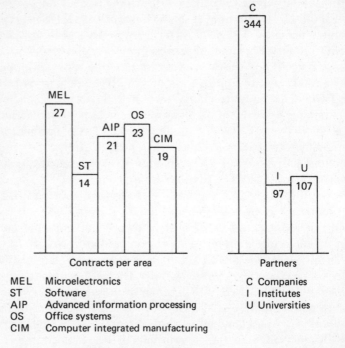

Figure 6   ESPRIT projects, 1984

Source: Mackintosh International, ESPRIT Conference, September 1984.

1983 a representative of Sony explained: 'Forget about technology. Anything Sony produces now anyone can replicate within weeks. The real key is the ability to market the product.' These critics of ESPRIT believed that what was necessary was a vehicle through which marketing and distribution ventures between Europe, Japan and the USA could be promoted. In addition, many doubted whether cooperative European research was in fact possible. Darryl Hooper, the Director of GEC's Hirst Research Laboratories in Wembley, told *New Scientist* (23 June 1983): 'My initial reaction was how to get something out of the programme, without giving secrets away to the other buggers.' Hooper did, however, feel that it was possible that ESPRIT might act as a catalyst, leading to substantially improved production techniques in European companies.

Whilst few of the big twelve IT companies concerned with the initial preparation of ESPRIT made such criticisms, critics of ESPRIT pointed out that since these companies stood to benefit substantially from ESPRIT backing, they were hardly likely to. The criticism which did come from some of these companies concerned ESPRIT funding. Klaus Luft, the Vice-President of Nixdorf, felt that the decision to limit Community funding to 50 per cent of the estimated project cost would deter the smaller companies. Luft commented that: 'Innovation is not just produced by large firms. To be successful, governments have to change the environment in taxation and legal terms.' Nevertheless, the Commission received not one request for more than 50 per cent funding from a small company in the 1984 and 1985 proposals.

A further criticism was that ESPRIT did not prohibit participation by non-European-owned multinationals such as IBM and ITT. Whilst there was no formal clause directly excluding such companies, the final terms of ESPRIT did impose certain restrictions, designed to ensure that, on the one hand, research was carried out at facilities within Europe, and, on the other, that the fruits of any research should not be transferred for development to divisions of multinationals located outside Europe.

Despite this, IBM publicized the fact that it could not restrict research results to its UK and European operations, and found both the European Commission and the computing press sympathetic to its position. *Computing* made the point on 23 October

1983 that: 'A widely dispersed production company sourcing different products in different countries could not seriously and honestly give such restrictive assurances: the proposition is untenable.'

Of the seven proposals IBM submitted in 1984 five passed the initial technical screening stage and were forwarded to the Management Committee for further evaluation. IBM was particularly anxious to participate in ESPRIT, since it realized that there were considerable benefits to be reaped from being seen as a European company, especially in the area of telecommunications.

The decision to allow non-European-owned multinationals based in Europe to participate in ESPRIT was largely technical, and one which Amedee Turner, MEP, and QC, considered to be almost inevitable:

> It is judicially and political impractical to exclude from ESPRIT joint ventures between European-based subsidiaries of American and Japanese multinationals. Indeed, the United States and Japan both fund British subsidiaries in their territories and Britain and Europe do not fund their subsidiaries outside their own territories. Of course, discretion must be used as to which joint ventures such companies would be admitted to: but it is not practical to exclude them on judicial grounds. (*House of Lords, op. cit.*)

A final criticism of ESPRIT was that it was not the right mechanism to bring about technology transfer. The Japanese experience in the VLSI research programme had shown that there were great benefits to be drawn from setting up a central laboratory. Companies such as ICL, Bull and Siemens felt that it would have been more appropriate for the Community to have established or encouraged industry-based research groupings aimed at creating centres of technological excellence. In particular, ICL felt that ESPRIT could have been used to give the initial impetus to the establishment of such centres, which would then have been allowed to determine the detailed specifications of the project themselves. The centre established in Munich by ICL, Bull and Siemens was cited as a possible example of this, although it was not a participant in the ESPRIT programme.

Although the ESPRIT programme was heavily dependent upon a large (50 per cent) public subsidy, it was not devised by a group of bureaucrats but was rather the result of a series of consultations firstly with the twelve largest European electronics companies and then many others. Not surprisingly, therefore, these companies were eager to participate in ESPRIT, which they saw as a means of achieving financial support for research which, in all likelihood, they would have undertaken anyway. They were also keen to gain government commitment to existing business strategy. As a consequence, the programme that emerged was a collection of company preferences.

The principal objective of ESPRIT was to encourage cooperation between companies in pre-competitive research. Yet, as we have seen from Chapter 3, companies were already beginning to realize the benefits of collaboration, not only in R&D but also at the production and marketing levels. Hence, whether public funds were necessary to encourage inter-company cooperation is questionable, particularly when one takes account of the fact that one of the most significant collaborative efforts, the Research Centre at Munich established by ICL, Bull and Siemens, took place outside the remit of ESPRIT.

When evaluating ESPRIT, it should be remembered that the Commission's powers were limited by the need to secure the cooperation of the member states. As was to be expected, member state governments were more concerned with promoting the interests of their national champions than they were about establishing a strategic plan for the radical rationalization and restructuring of the European IT industry. The fact that the Community remains a collection of sovereign states means that Europe as a single market remains at a considerable disadvantage compared with the unified markets of Japan and the USA.

An analysis of the European response cannot be completed by examining the Community response alone. As the member states are still essentially sovereign, possessing the powers to pursue their own policies, it is important to look at what took place at the national level within Europe. In the following chapter we shall therefore examine the behaviour of the one member state in particular – Britain.

5 The British Response

The initiative for the British Fifth Generation Computer Project came from a small group of computer science academics. Early in 1981, on learning of the dangerous threat presented by the imminent Japanese programme, Tony Hoare of Oxford University, Bob Kowalski of Imperial College, London, and Donald Michie of Edinburgh University, took it upon themselves to write to the Department of Industry (DoI) to suggest that these Tokyo developments, and their implications, should be the subject of a thorough investigation. This letter went without reply. In September 1981 the DoI received an invitation from MITI to send observers to the conference with marked the launch of their Fifth Generation Computer Programme. Despite this earlier concern shown by Hoare, Kowalski and Michie, the ministry turned to other British academics, asking, among others, Roger Needham of Cambridge University, Brian Randell of Newcastle University and Philip Treleaven of Reading, if they would be prepared to attend the MITI conference, and then, in the light of their findings, report back to the government on what they considered to be appropriate strategies for the British to adopt. The academics were joined on the trip by Ron Atkinson of the DoI. The conspicuous absence of industrialists was at the request of the Japanese.

When the British team returned to London, the academics concerned considered a mere statement of fact or description of Japan's Fifth Generation activities to be inappropriate, and together with sixteen academics who worked together on the Science and Engineering Research Council (SERC) compiled a document which proposed that £350m should be made available for research specifically in VLSI, Man Machine Interface (MMI), software engineering, and, notwithstanding the recommendations of the 1973 Lighthill Report, Artificial Intelligence (AI). The Lighthill Report had proposed that AI, being intellectually out of fashion in the UK, looked undeserving of public funding at the time of the report. However, the fact that Japan planned to invest substantially in this area led the British team to reconsider, and

57

realize the potential of AI. Hence, AI, or Intelligent Knowledge Based Systems (IKBS), as it was now relabelled, was included as one of the four areas of suggested research.

These recommendations were passed on to a conference of British industrialists, academics and civil servants, in London in January 1982. The scale and cohesiveness of the Japanese programme, together with the danger of an American response, were seen by those attending the conference as a major competitive threat to the British electronics industry. The conference therefore called for an urgent study into the scope for possible collaboration in the UK, geared to Britain's particular strengths and requirements. However, although on the whole the industrialists attending the conference were reasonably satisfied with the academics' recommendations, they did not necessarily consider the academic profession to be the most appropriate for making these sorts of decisions. In particular, they felt that academics were not always able to understand and appreciate the needs of industry, and the importance of research applications.

The DoI responded to the conference recommendations by setting up the Alvey Committee, which was initially composed entirely of industrialists from established British electronics companies, including British Telecom (BT), GEC, Plessey and Ferranti, although one academic, Roger Needham, was later coopted. Surprisingly, in spite of being aware of Japan's ambitious plans in this area, Alvey did not include any members of the British AI community.

Within three months the Alvey Committee had developed an extensive research programme (covering the four main areas of MMI, VLSI, IKBS and software engineering), but because of the speed with which this had been compiled, certain crucial areas were neglected. In particular, no attempt had been made to investigate thoroughly, as the Japanese had done between 1979 and 1981, what future users' requirements of IT would be. Although advice from industry had been sought, and 115 submissions received, as Frank Lands, a systems analyst at the LSE, later pointed out, only three of these were from users and, consequently (with the exception of the MoD), the Alvey Programme was dominated by the views of British electronics producers. In addition, the Computer Services Association (CSA), representing software companies, was particularly critical of the absence of an overall short, medium or long-term national strategy for IT and applications. One of its representatives commented that:

> The CSA's companies are concentrating on the market place. A relatively small company has brought out an expert system for conveyancing – something which there is a clear market for. It is at the nitty-gritty applications end that software companies are working. Alvey offers nothing for them.

In their defence of the Alvey Programme, Committee members stressed that their brief was to propose a programme of research in Advanced Information Technology, and that to have looked at the market would have been to exceed their terms of reference. Computer architecture was not initially isolated as a separate research area. This decision was supported by Ian Barron (Managing Director of Inmos), who argued that architecture should underlie the whole Alvey Programme on pragmatic and organisational grounds. Barron later decided that this had been a mistake and that architecture should be separately investigated. Because Britain was thought to be in a competitively weak market position in memory chips and storage, the Committee fundamentally rejected the inclusion of research in these areas within the programme.

The programme, established within the space of three months, inevitably represented a compromise between different sectional interests. However, the inclusion of the proposed VLSI research proved to be the most contentious issue. Several members argued that, since chip research was extremely expensive, and as 90 per cent of the market had already been captured by Japan and the USA, the funds would be more efficiently employed in areas where Britain had a greater chance of successfully capturing a reasonable market share. On the other hand, those in favour of VLSI argued that it was a core-enabling technology of IT, and as such was not an area Britain could afford to neglect if she was going to sharpen her competitive edge in the 1980s. A further factor contributing to the inclusion of VLSI was that provision had already been made in the ESPRIT programme for research in this area. However, of paramount importance was the fact that the

MoD (which was later to be made a partner in the Alvey Directorate) began to show considerable interest in VLSI, which meant that its inclusion became almost inevitable.

The IKBS section of the report was greatly facilitated by the fact that IKBS had previously been the subject of an SERC study. However, this section of the report was later criticized for being too academic, and adopting too long-term an approach for an industrial R&D programme. It bore the closest relationship in technical content to the Japanese Fifth Generation proposals.

The software engineering side of the programme was split into two sections: the work on formal methods, which was to be dominated by a number of SERC projects, most of which were already in progress by the time the Alvey Report was written; and the work on tools, which came under the influence of companies working on large real time systems for MoD and BT contracts. This effectively meant that the software engineering programme had very little, if anything, to do with Britain's software houses, a number of which were later to express their disillusion at having in effect been excluded from the programme.

The MMI section of the programme, which, like IKBS, had been included largely through imitation of the Japanese, proved to be the most difficult to develop, since it covered a very broad, heterogeneous field, with no clearly defined objectives, and was further hampered by the distinct lack of competent British MMI experts. Whilst the majority of the committee agreed that MMI should be included as part of the programme, the shortage of skilled personnel led many to express strong reservations about Britain's chances of success in this field.

After much internal debate, the Alvey Committee submitted its report to the Department of Industry in September 1982, recommending a five-year £350m programme, based on collaboration between industry, academia, and three government departments: the DoI (or DTI as it was shortly to become), MoD and DES (acting through the SERC). The Committee held that:

> [The Japanese] have correctly identified the major advances in the technology which will be necessary to achieve [a series of objectives including the application of IT to areas of society where increases in efficiency and productivity could be most

beneficial] and we believe they are right in identifying that the magnitude of the advances required is such that collaboration in the necessary research is essential.

The report argued that the case for a British collaborative programme rested upon five main propositions:

First, the world IT market is one of major growth. The UK needs to capture the largest possible share of this market, but on current trends our share will decline. (As presented in *A Strategy for Information Technology*: a report to the NEB by Pactel, 1981.) Secondly, a necessary, though not sufficient, condition for reversing this trend and increasing our world market penetration is that we have competitive levels of achievement in certain fundamental enabling technologies. Thirdly, these enabling technologies, and the infrastructure and systems which connect and exploit them, can be identified now. Fourth, we require a strong domestic capability in these technologies since we cannot depend upon other countries supplying them. Fifthly, to achieve the capability a national collaborative effort is required. This means government backing.

The report recommended that a new directorate responsible for implementing the programme should be established within the Department of Industry, and that the programme should run as a UK effort:

Foreign multinationals should participate only where they can contribute a particular asset vital to the programme; where the results of their involvement will be available to the benefit of UK industry as a whole; and where it is guaranteed that valuable technical information will not leak from the UK.

The Alvey Committee's report caused considerable interdepartmental Whitehall conflict. Mrs Thatcher refused to accept the report when it was first presented to Cabinet, in March 1983, and the Treasury had hastily to erase references to the programme in the Chancellor's April budget. Mrs Thatcher eventually agreed to

Source: *New Scientist*, 12 April 1984.

the programme in April 1983, but only on condition that the maximum level of government funding for the industry parts of the project should be 50 per cent, not 90 per cent.

The Alvey Committee had proposed 90 per cent government funding for those parts of the programme covering longer-term industrial research work, to avoid the 'free-rider' problem, and exclusion rights difficulties, arguing that otherwise it would be extremely difficult to persuade industry's experts to work on projects whose results were to be made freely available. In addition, attention was drawn to the fact that in Japan MITI was providing 100 per cent funding for the Fifth Generation Project (although firms still paid salaries for staff seconded to ICOT), and in the USA the Strategic Computing Initiative was being funded through DARPA at 100 per cent.

The decision to reduce the level of government funding from 90 per cent to a maximum of 50 per cent profoundly influenced the implementation of the Alvey programme. In particular, it reduced the possibility of small-firm participation, and, since those firms which provided 50 per cent of the funds were to retain the property rights, the possibility of research generating industry-wide benefits through the dissemination of innovations and inventions seemed less likely. Furthermore, it was argued that, because of the nature and characteristics of the software industry, these financial arrangements would create particular difficulties for the software engineering element of the programme; basically, the firms which had been responsible for the development of the Alvey software strategy were too busily engaged in the pursuit of income from their service work to be able to make the sort of long-term, uncertain and risky investment the 50 per cent clause required. The 50 per cent programme was thus thought by its administrators to have shorter horizons and less coherence than would have been possible with 90 per cent funding.

Although there were those who considered the Alvey Directorate to be 'technically unqualified' and 'bureaucratic', the severist criticisms of Alvey, from both industry and academia, were provoked by the funding issue. One member of the Alvey Committee lamented the fact that the change to 50 per cent, from 90 per cent, funding meant that the Alvey Directorate could not place an order with contracting companies. It was left instead to make do with 'trying to connect together the various odds and sods which interested companies are concerned to do.' Even those Alvey members who were sympathetic towards Mrs Thatcher – 'I can see why the government would be reluctant to give 90% funding for anything to a company like GEC', one commented – felt that by being asked to provide half the resources for projects companies were being given too much freedom to dictate the pattern of Alvey research. A leading industrialist later expressed the opinion that:

> Alvey is less control by direction, and more by what the companies want to do ... Alvey should have taken the lead in formulating industrial strategy. It was a mistake to leave it to the participating firms. We need a definite strategy, not a pious hope.

These same sentiments were echoed by a member of GEC:

> It is not good enough for Alvey to be driven by what the upswell of opinion thinks is needed. It must be determined to carry out

a particular programme of action. Otherwise, it will just be a dripping tap of pump-priming money, much of which will undoubtedly go to waste.

Many industrialists within the IT community refused to believe that the Alvey effort was actually bringing in new money, since the funds had, after all, been raised from the MoD, DTI and SERC's resources. One industrialist wryly commented: 'No new money was found for Alvey, it was simply formed by a realloction of MoD, SERC and DTI money. Thus, it is not a genuine national IT effort.'

A considerable number of academics, especially at Edinburgh University and Imperial College, London, where substantial new work was being undertaken due to Alvey, were critical of the fact that Alvey contracts did not offer any overhead funding. As a consequence, many participating academic institutions found themselves running very short of offices and laboratories.

Furthermore, several members of the Alvey Directorate felt frustrated by the speed with which Alvey funds had been allocated, in an attempt to avoid the programme becoming a victim of government cutbacks, and thought that if Alvey was to stand a chance of being successful, greater flexibility in the distribution of funds was essential. As one of the members of the Directorate commented:

> There is a need to keep money uncommitted until users are ready to apply for it. This contrasts strongly with Whitehall's normal practice of snatching money back at the end of the financial year if it has not been spent. Alvey as a whole has no unallocated budget line because the Treasury could not cope with this idea.

There were also those who felt that with three-quarters of Alvey's funds being monopolized by the large, established electronics companies, such as Plessey, GEC and Ferranti (which had been on the Alvey Committee), the money available was being seriously misallocated. One member of the venture capital community commented that, 'Alvey is funding projects in the big

companies which would have been done anyway', and a member
of GEC privately admitted:

> GEC is in a position to fund its own research, and will only take
> part in Alvey or ESPRIT if the latter covers areas of research
> which GEC would have undertaken anyway. Fifty percent
> funding in such instances, is better than no funding at all.

This led one member of the British Technology Group (BTG) to
argue that the Alvey Directorate had taken the easy course in
directing funds into large companies: 'They knew (the big companies') track records. It takes far longer to make an investment in
a small company.'

In addition, there were those (mainly venture capitalists) who
felt that the financial arrangements had in effect created a 'Catch
22' situation: on the one hand, it could be argued that minimizing
government support might reduce the possibility of failure: 'Anyone who was going to do a piece of research would do it anyway,
with or without government support. If they wouldn't do the
research without support, then it's a non-starter.' On the other
hand, it could, with equal validity, be argued that the financial

Source: *New Scientist*, 7 February 1985.

arrangements were designed to maximize the likelihood of failure: 'They give money to ten companies and spread the risk: this may guarantee ten failures. Nine because they shouldn't have been given the money in the first place, and the tenth because it was only given 10% of the funding.'

The Alvey Directorate was aware that the greatest proportion of its funds was being allocated to the large companies, and was anxious to encourage smaller firms to apply, particularly in MMI, IKBS and software engineering, where unlike VLSI, the cost of essential equipment was not as prohibitive. Despite this, all four research areas continued to be dominated by Plessey, GEC, STC, Racal and Ferranti.

Although the Alvey Directorate, despite shortages of skilled manpower, found little difficulty in achieving cooperation between the larger firms, Brian Oakley frequently indicated that the key question, as he saw it, was whether this cooperation would survive the R&D stage, since he believed that collaboration between companies and universities was an essential prerequisite for the building of a successful Fifth Generation Computer programme. Oakley also hoped, although this was considered by industrialists and venture capitalists to be highly unlikely, that the collaboration which had been established would extend to the manufacture and marketing of products. One member of the BTG recalled a joint venture instigated in 1968 by Tony Benn (then Minister of Technology), in which Ferranti, Plessey and Marconi collaborated in a £5m publicly funded microelectronics research programme. As with Alvey, it had been reasonably straightforward to persuade the companies to collaborate on the engineering side, but when it came to marketing the product, it was a completely different story. In Japan, too, it was accepted in government circles that while companies could be induced to cooperate in R&D, they could not be expected to be anything but fiercely competitive in the market place. However, the Alvey Directorate remained unconvinced by these arguments, and optimistic that cooperation might be extended beyond the R&D stage.

The beneficial cooperation Alvey had established between industry and academia was one of the most popular and widely praised aspects of the programme, reflected thus in the words of one industrialist:

The one rock solid gain from Alvey is the change in climate it has brought about. For small companies to be involved in the research community would have been unthinkable only three years ago. Now bodies like the Medical Research Council and the Imperial Cancer Research Fund are falling over themselves to cooperate with software companies.

In spite of this, there were those who felt that collaboration could create severe problems, particularly in situations where four or five participants were engaged in a project which seemed unlikely to succeed unless the objectives were modified and less ambitious goals set.

The industry–university collaboration did, however, create serious administrative problems for the Alvey Directorate. Since it was left to determine the division of industrial property rights (IPR) and the terms of collaboration, it ran into many difficulties. The Alvey Directorate could not offer model agreements in the first instance, since it was felt that too many issues of principle were involved. Hence, for many universities and companies, the experience of drawing up such collaborative agreements was a precedent that could not be rushed into lightly. Inevitably these bureaucratic negotiations delayed the issuing and signing of contracts.

In addition to the financial criticisms and reservations expressed about the possibility of successful collaboration, the software companies were extremely dissatisfied with the vague and often confused direction given by the Alvey Directorate. As one industrialist explained:

[Alvey] says it's about IT, but if one looks at what it is supporting, there is a great difference between Alvey and the users. When the strategy paper was put forward on software engineering, I was puzzled as to whom it was aimed at. I wasn't sure whether it was only the MoD and BT that it was serving, or whether it was genuinely supposed to have a wider remit which included data processing departments.

Furthermore, certain software houses felt that Alvey was too academic, too concerned with supporting the big companies, and too slow working. Moreover, the SERC policy, initiated in 1980, of reducing the IT budget by 25 per cent over a three-year period, raised criticism from all quarters and was explicitly attacked in the Alvey Report. It was felt that this strategy would reduce the number of IT postgraduates to an unacceptably low level, which in turn could seriously damage Alvey's chances of success. One academic remarked: 'Politicians should be careful to get a proper ramp up of support for a project, even if it means allowing funds out in advance.'

As the Alvey scheme progressed, the direction of Public funding for IT in general changed in emphasis, away from helping IT as such and towards encouraging mature industries to introduce IT. This caused concern within the IT industry, despite the fact that the change was aimed at a user community. A member of BT commented:

> In early discussions with Alvey representatives we were assured that the pre-competitive nature of collaboration would be boosted by MISP [Microelectronics Industry Support Programme] money to support transfer to volume production. We are now very concerned by the Government's re-evaluation of the role of MISP, and the detrimental knock-on effects of an apparent lack of confidence in electronics on the part of the government. Generally, the effect of uncertainty is to put a brake on the design of really competitive products.

But, even he was forced to admit that there was a certain logic to the government's action. 'Generally speaking, caution is necessary when considering the market and impact of new IT services. They are commonly oversold.'

Towards the end of its second year, concern was expressed, particularly by ICL, that Alvey was failing to keep abreast of changing needs in this fiercely competitive area of IT, and similar views were expressed by one member of BT:

> I'm concerned that Alvey does not fully appreciate that the rest of the world is moving on, as we attempt to catch up. The committee of academics and industrialists whose work led to

the founding of Alvey targetted competitiveness to be attained by 1987. I think the time-scale slippage to 1989 is now too late.

Throughout this chapter we have seen that, although Alvey took over many projects which were already under way or which were about to begin, the slow turning wheels of bureaucracy delayed Britain's IT effort considerably.

Despite the fact that the British government, through procurement and industrial policies, was significantly more powerful than the European Commission, Alvey was basically a carbon copy of ESPRIT. It had the same objective of encouraging pre-competitive R&D between companies; like ESPRIT, it aimed at providing participating companies with 50 per cent grants, and finally it was to be administered similarly, by awarding contracts on the basis of promising proposals, if and when these arrived. However, whereas Alvey was concerned only with encouraging cooperation between British companies and institutions, ESPRIT had the more ambitious, perhaps less attainable, goal of fostering cooperation between different member states.

Because the Alvey programme lacked selectivity, British companies were encouraged to collaborate with each other in areas of technological backwardness. In these areas collaboration with Japanese or American companies would have been strategically more advantageous. The inclusion of VLSI was particularly contentious, and one member of Plessey commented that, 'even if Alvey's objectives in VLSI are completely fulfilled, we will still be two to three years behind the Japanese and American competition.' As with ESPRIT, Alvey was criticized for having allowed the participating companies to dominate discussions, and consequently for allowing the programme which emerged to have limited horizons.

Since our examination of both ESPRIT and Alvey has highlighted the preoccupation which European governments had with promoting cooperation between domestic companies, in the chapter that follows we shall investigate the strategies adopted by European companies throughout the early 1980s, and see to what extent they were compatible with those being pursued at the public level.

6 Strategies of European IT Companies in the 1980s

The major electronics IT companies of Japan, the USA, Europe and the UK, being multinationals with global strategies, are not constrained in their activities by national boundaries, and while they have often been prepared to participate in government programmes, as a means of securing financial assistance, this has not prevented them from sacrificing the potential sucess of these schemes by collaborating or competing with each other. Certain companies, in an attempt to conquer opponents and win the IT war, have adopted a two-stage strategy, whereby they actively pursue cooperation with competitors to strengthen their position in the short run but only in order to obliterate these competitors turned partners in the long run. It is the economic, political and strategic motives behind these international alliances, together with their implications for national IT policies, which form the subject matter of this penultimate chapter.

Here the strategies of selected major European electronics companies are the principal focus of attention, since, although the American and Japanese chapters involved considerable discussion of company strategies, the British and European chapters focused almost exclusively upon the Alvey and ESPRIT programmes. By examining European company strategies before and during the establishment of Alvey and ESPRIT, one is able to drew comparisons between these and the public policies of the British government and the Commission.

Since the Second World War several changes in both the nature of, and driving force behind, these moves towards international collaboration have been witnessed. Although in the immediate post-war period Britain reigned supreme in the computer field, with many American companies, including IBM, avidly chasing licences for British components, by the mid-1950s the scales had been tilted in favour of America, which, until the Japanese challenge in the mid-1970s, took over the dominant position in computer technology. Initially, during the 1950s and 1960s, the Japanese had relied heavily upon American licences; however, by the mid-1970s they were already beginning to show signs of technological superiority, particularly in microchips.

By the 1980s the hegemony of America, coupled with this emerging Japanese superiority, led European companies to abandon their 1960s' and 1970s' strategy of pursuing American-independent technology, and to consider seriously adopting common international, if not American (i.e. IBM), technological standards.

The Japanese Fifth Generation Computer Programme, and the imitative projects in America, Britain and Europe, were all part of the international battle for technological superiority (and one closely associated with standards), which was considered by certain members of the IT community to be a prerequisite for market success. An alternative school of thought held that the battle over future technology was a sideshow, designed to divert attention and resources away from the ever-present and very real battle raging over market shares, and argued that cooperation with foreign companies, especially with those operating in a different rather than competing branch of the IT field, was a more efficient strategy than that of fighting a relentless and wasteful technological battle.

One of the companies adopting this collaborative philosophy was ICL, whose original 1970s' policy of producing, largely for the public sector, non-IBM-compatible computers was seen to have been fatally flawed, since it had made the company almost totally dependent upon the government's preferential purchasing policy, and, at the turn of the decade, when government expenditure was severely restricted, ICL was driven to the verge of collapse.

In the 1980s, faced with falling hardware sales revenues (but increasing returns on software), ICL decided to rationalize its hardware business severely, shedding 860 workers in 1980 alone, and began giving priority to marketing strategies by establishing dealer networks. The new board of managers, appointed in 1981, decided that if a comprehensive range of products was to be offered, ICL would have to look beyond in-house capability and instead forge alliances with companies possessing different technological expertise. Accordingly, an agreement with Fujitsu, one of the world's leaders in semiconductor technology, was signed. This proved to be extremely beneficial for ICL, providing the company with access to VLSI circuits, without the attendant R&D costs. ICL also teamed up with Mitel, a Canadian telecommunications equipment manufacturer, to market the Mitel SX 2000 digital PABX (Private Branch Exchange) in the UK. But, because of problems Mitel experienced with its software development programme, this relationship did not develop as planned, and instead ICL turned to the massive AT&T for help. AT&T had been released by the US government from its international marketing constraints, and was, during the early 1980s, actively seeking marketing partners in Europe. The American company was very responsive to the British company's overtures, and on 15 May 1984 ICL announced its intention of cooperating with AT&T in the development of a value-added network in the UK.

ICL's 'hand of friendship' also extended to her European neighbours. In addition to participating in the ESPRIT Programme, the company agreed with Siemens of West Germany and Bull of France to set up a joint research centre in Munich for the development of IT technologies.

For ICL, both the Alvey and ESPRIT programmes provided only a partial solution to the company's problems; collaboration with American and Japanese companies was seen as an essential ingredient in the recipe for success, and, even after the merger with STC in 1984, a significant determinant of the company's strategy throughout the 1980's. (For a list of ICL's joint ventures during this period, see Table 10.)

Italy's Olivetti, though starting from a stronger position and exhibiting a more vigorous and confident marketing policy, followed an approach similar to that of ICL. Olivetti's chief executive, Carlo de Benedetti, believed that forging links with other high technology companies was the only way a company of Olivetti's relatively modest size could keep abreast of advanced developments, while concentrating its own R&D in specialist areas. In addition to concluding a number of important agreements for cooperative R&D, manufacturing and marketing, Benedetti stimulated the creation of a venture capital fund which was later used to buy

Table 10   ICL's joint ventures, 1980–4

Company	Country	Purpose
Collaboration entered into by ICL		
Fujitsu	Japan	Technical exchange, large computers
Logica	UK	Collaboration on DRS 8801
Sinclair Research	UK	Integrated terminal/phone
Bull	France	Joint Research Centre
Siemens	Germany	Joint Research Centre
Rair	US	Marketing personal computer
AT&T	US	Cooperation VANS and telecommunications
PERQ Systems	US	Scientific small computers
Mitel	Canada	Marketing PABX

Company	Country	Product area
Acquisitions and investments		
Computer Leasing	UK	Computer leasing
CADCentre*	UK	CAD/CAM
PERQ Systems*	US	Scientific workstations

*Part ownership.

equity in American high-tech firms. This provided Olivetti with a means of keeping a watchful eye on developments in American technology (see Table 11).

In 1980, in an attempt to create a powerful European competitor for the world market in data processing and office automation, Olivetti sold 33 per cent of its equity to the French company Saint Gobain. However, after Saint Gobain was nationalized by the Mitterrand government in 1982 (and subsequently forced to leave the electronics market), cooperation on both sides deteriorated. On 18 October 1983, urged by Benedetti, the French sold two-thirds of their holding back to Olivetti, giving the remaining third to CIT-Alcatel. This led to a new collaborative agreement between Olivetti and CIT-Alcatel for the development of a new generation of electronic typewriters.

By 1983 Benedetti had become convinced that European collaborations were not enough and that a link-up with a major American company was in Olivetti's long-term interest. Olivetti had experimented with an American link-up in 1982, when it had

Table 11   Olivetti's venture capital investments 1980–84

Company	Country	Production area
Applied Micro Circuit	US	MOS ICs
Compuscan	US	Office Automation
Data Terminal Systems	US	Point-of-sale terminals
Docutel Olivetti	US	Bank equipment, cash dispensers
Intecom	US	Advanced PABX
IPL	US	Plug-compatible computers
Irwin Olivetti	US	High density discs
Ithaca Intersysts	US	Micros, graphics terminals
Lanx	US	Magnetic discs
Stratus Computer	US	Mini-computers
Syntrex	US	Word processors
Telxon	US	Portable terminals
Transactional Management	US	Point-of-sale terms
Lee Data	US	Display terminals
Linear Tech	US	Linear circuits
MicroOffice Systems	US	Portable terminals
Prolink	US	Office automation
VLSI Technology	US	ICs
Filex	US	Electronic file systems
MicroAge	US	Computer stores chain
Shared Financial Systems	US	Software house
Corona	US	Medical computers
Hermes Precisa Int.	Switzerland	Peripherals and distribution
Logabox	France	Office equipment

merged Olivetti (USA) with one of its venture capital investments (Docutel, a Dallas-based manufacturer of automatic tellers). However, whilst this small-scale venture had been moderately successful, it was not enough to satiate Benedetti's appetite for a larger slice of the American market and, in the 1984 company accounts, he wrote:

> The anticipated global competition can be effectively met only through functional coalitions between companies on a world scale, making available structures which are fully com-

plementary as regards both the control of technologies and production applications, and the effective and complete coverage of markets and services at a world level. . . . In view of this, an alliance with AT&T was the inevitable choice to enable Olivetti to retain its own leadership and to enter the present evolution process, as a global competitor in terms of products and market coverage.

Accordingly, Benedetti finalized an agreement whereby 25 per cent of Olivetti was sold to AT&T. The latter agreed to market Olivetti's personal computers in the US, in return for which Olivetti would sell AT&T's telecommunications systems throughout Europe. Both companies also agreed to exchange product licences and to cooperate in the joint development of new products. By this means Olivetti secured direct access to AT&T's Bell Laboratories, the world's largest telecommunications research centre. Although the deal infuriated the French and threatened to upset Olivetti's relationship with Docutel, it led to a rapid increase in Olivetti's exports to the USA, with an estimated first year revenue of $250m.

A further link in Olivetti's chain of agreements was added when, in June 1985, a technology exchange agreement was secured with Toshiba. In a deal similar to that with AT&T, a proportion of Olivetti (Japan) was sold to Toshiba as a means of securing the partnership. Finally in 1985 Olivetti stepped in to take a share in the ailing British microcomputer manufacturer Acorn. This gave Olivetti access to an extended customer base in Britain. (For a summary of Olivetti's joint ventures, see Table 12.)

Following the election of the Mitterrand government in 1981, the principal French electronics companies found themselves almost powerless to operate independently of the Socialist government's ambitious industrial policy, which aimed at completely rationalizing and restructuring the French electronics industry. During the presidency of Giscard d'Estaing, Thomson had been persuaded, with largely disastrous results, to diversify into telecommunications, microcomputers and semiconductors; but, when under the Socialist regime the newly elected chairman of Thomson, Alain Gomez, announced his intention of selling off the troubled electronics division, Compagnie Générale de Radiologie (CGR), he was prevented from so doing, since this was considered to be against the new government's plan. The Socialists' industrial

Table 12   Collaboration entered into by Olivetti, 1980–5

Company	Country	Purpose
Toshiba	Japan	Technology exchange
Sharp	Japan	Fast copying machines
Hitachi	Japan	Computer marketing pact
Acorn	UK	Microcomputer deal
Plessey	UK	Licence to make PABXs
CIT-Alcatel	France	R&D in typewriters
Northern Telecom	Canada	Licence to make PABXs
Digital Research	US	Software marketing
Kyocera	US	OEM agreement in ICs
Intel	US	OEM agreement in ICs
Xerox	US	Technology exchange
AT&T	US	Marketing and technology exchange

strategy also created severe financial problems for Thomson. With the curbs on public sector spending introduced in 1983, Gomez found himself forced to plan Thomson's future investment on the assumption that private sector finances would be essential. Accordingly, in late 1983, Gomez split Thomson into five subsidiaries, each of which, when profitable, would be in a position to go public, and in May 1984, heralding a positive move towards the private sector, the company announced that it would offer approximately $100m worth of bond convertible equity to raise the capital for its investment programme.

Although creating certain difficulties, the French government did encourage the electronics companies by giving them R&D and reorganisation subsidies (see Table 13), and although in the early 1980s it was forced to accept that it was too late to catch up with the world's semiconductor and data-processing leaders, it did feel that if Europe's strength in telecommunications, particularly public exchanges, was pooled, outside competitors could be beaten off effectively. Accordingly, the telecommunications activities of Thomson and CIT-Alcatel were merged, creating a monopoly supplier of telecommunications equipment in France. In its attempt to build a strong, united European electronics industry, with French companies at its heart, the French government, despite arousing the suspicions of both the West German cartels

Table 13   French government grants and Thomson's collaborative ventures

Aid to French state-owned electronics companies, 1982–4, millions of francs			
Company	1982	1983	1984
Thomson	–	550	1,000
Thomson Telecom	–	–	700
Bull	–	1,500	1,000
CGE	–	150	–
Saint Gobain	–	–	150

Source: *The Economist*, 10 March 1984.

Collaborative ventures entered into by Thomson, 1980–4		
Company	Country	Purpose
Matsushita/JVC	Japan	Manufacture of VHS VCRs
Thorn EMI	UK	Manufacture of VHS VCRs
Telefunken	Germany	Consumer electronics
Philips	Netherlands	Marketing home computer
Philips	Netherlands	Common standards for DBS
Motorola	USA	Production of Components
Fortune Computer	USA	Production of micros
Eagle Computer	USA	Production of micros
Xerox	USA	Optical disks
General Inst	USA	Optical fibres
Hughes	USA	Satellites
Diasonics	USA	R&D sale medical equipment

office and Europe's largest consumer electronics company, Philips, encouraged Thomson to bid firstly, though unsuccessfully, for the West German consumer electronics giant Grundig, and later, with success, for Telefunken, the consumer electronics subsidiary of the troubled AEG electronics group.

Although the consumer electronics giant Philips, with an annual R&D budget of $1 billion in the 1980s (a figure exceeded only by IBM and AT&T), had for nearly a century prided itself upon pursuing independent technological development, by the 1980s the

Table 14   Philips' joint ventures and acquisitions, 1980–4

	Collaborative ventures entered into	
Company	*Country*	*Purpose*
Matsushita	Japan	Manufacture of VHS VCRs
Sony	Japan	Development of CD-ROM
Control Data	USA	Work on optical storage
RCA	USA	Development of ICs
Intel	USA	Development of ICs
Texas Instruments	USA	Development of ICs
AT&T	USA	Digital 'phone exchanges
Warner	USA	Pre-recorded sound pact
Atari	USA	Development of video game
CIT-Alcatel	France	Work on mobile 'phones
Thomson	France	Marketing home computer
Bull	France	Development of smart card
AEG consortium	Germany	Manufacture glass fibres
Siemens	Germany	Development of ICs
Racal	UK	Work on mobile 'phones

	Acquisitions	
Company	*Country*	*Production area*
General Telephone & Electric Corp	USA	TVs and components
Westinghouse Electric Corp	USA	Lamps division
VALTEC	USA	Optical fibres and wiring
Compagnie des Lampes	France	Lamps
Grundig	Germany	Consumer electronics

company recognised that, given the speed and intensity of the IT race, collaboration could prove to be an extremely beneficial strategy. Hence, in 1982, Wisse Dekker, Philips' new chairman, who was one of the most vociferous protagonists of the ESPRIT programme, initiated a policy deliberately designed to reverse the earlier isolationist stance (see Table 14).

However, whilst Philips' productivity in consumer electronics increased during the early 1980s, the flood of Japanese imports caused sales to lag behind, forcing further rationalization and coordination of production. For example, at one point Philips found itself producing 300 different models of black and white television sets.

The most radical of Philips' changes came in the mid-1980s, with its capitulation to the Japanese on Video Cassette Recorder (VCR) standards. An essential ingredient in Philips' strategy before the 1980s had been the development of new products, which were ultimately successful in setting industry standards, enabling the company to avoid both licensing problems and difficulties in acquiring the use of foreign patents. However, 1980–4 saw the failure of Philips' V2000 VCR. Despite having 'invented the VCR, Philips found, by the time it launched its model, that JVC's VHS and Sony's Betamax standards already dominated the industry, and although Philips won a 20 per cent share of the West German market, it managed to capture only 1 per cent of the lucrative VCR trade in Britain, and in November 1983 was forced to conclude a licensing agreement with JVC for the manufacture of VHS machines.

Because the management of Philips considered success in IT to be dependent upon success in consumer electronics, it was anxious to expand its share of the European consumer electronics market. After having successfully frustrated Thomson's attempt, it proceeded to buy Grundig, and despite pressing for the development of a strong European electronics industry, concluded its own telecommunications agreement with AT&T.

The British electronics giant Thorn EMI was also anxious to find collaborators, and between 1980 and 1984 dramatically increased its participation in joint ventures (see Table 15). Thorn EMI already had an arrangement with the Swedish firm Ericsson to market its telecommunications equipment in Britain; to this it added contracts with JVC and AEG for the manufacture of VHS VCRs, and with C-Cov Electronics of the USA for the development of cable television.

The management of Thorn EMI, under Peter Laister, was also anxious, between 1983 and 1984, to reduce the company's reliance and dependence upon both consumer electronics and the UK market, and with this objective in mind endeavoured to buy British Aerospace (BAe). However, GEC, considering such an alliance to be unpalatable, forced Thorn EMI to abandon its plans

Table 15   Thorn EMI's joint ventures and acquisitions, 1980–4

Company	Collaboration entered into	
	Country	Purpose
Matsushita/JVC	Japan	Manufacture of VHS VCRs
Toshiba	Japan	Consumer electronics deal
Sony	Japan	Sale compact disc player
Thomson	France	Manufacture of VHS VCRs
AEG-Telefunken	Germany	Manufacture of VHS VCRs
Polly Peck	Turkey	Assembly and sale of CTVs
C-Corr	USA	Cable and TV licence

Company	Production and sales contracts for other firms	
	Country	Purpose
IBM	USA	Manufacture chip boards
TeleVideo	USA	Distribution of micros
Sinclair	UK	Manufacture micro-computers

Company	Acquisitions	
	Country	Production area
Software Sciences	UK	Software house
System Simulation	UK	Software house
Datasolve	UK	Computer bureau
Hazmac Handling	UK	Robotics, automation manufacture
Inmos	UK	Microchip plant

by entering into negotiations with BAe, although these later proved fruitless.

During the 1980s, at a time when many British companies were suffering from the recession, GEC, largely because of the buoyancy of the defence market following a 3 per cent per annum real increase in military expenditure, prospered. However, GEC's comfortable profits from defence led many to argue that the company was missing valuable opportunities in other areas of the IT industry. Although in 1981 GEC did form an information systems division, competition proved to be too fierce, profits were disappointing, a series of management upheavals followed, and in October 1984 it was announced that the division was to be disbanded.

GEC's attempts to expand into overseas markets, by acquiring foreign companies, were similarly unsuccessful (see Table 16). In 1982 Lord Weinstock, armed with GEC's large cash mountain, failed to acquire the ailing West German company AEG, which in 1983 was rescued by a consortium of German banks, and in the rationalization which followed Thomson was the sole beneficiary.

Despite its profitability, many considered that heavy dependence upon public sector procurement put GEC in a rather tenuous position, particularly with BT's imminent privatization. Following the entry into the UK market of the North American companies Mitel and Harris Corporation, the price of PABX's fell by 50 per cent, and delays in the joint development of the System X digital telephone exchange by GEC and Plessey led British Telecom to consider placing 25 per cent of the contracts for the rewiring of Britain's ageing communications network with foreign companies. Furthermore, doubts over the security of GEC's profitable defence business were cast when, in 1985, the Public Expenditure White Paper announced that cost-plus defence contracts, which had guaranteed companies a fixed return in addition to a 100 per cent subsidy of the R&D costs, were to cease.

The fall in interest rates between 1982 and 1984 provoked GEC's management into considering alternative tax-effective means of utilizing its cash mountain, and towards the end of 1984 the decision was taken to buy back 9 per cent of the company's own shares. This infuriated many of the smaller British electronics companies, who felt that, at such a crucial time, these resources should have been channelled into R&D. It was not until 1986 that GEC eventually found a company to invest some of its surplus cash in; it merged with Plessey.

While the performance of many European electronics companies may have been disappointing throughout the 1980s, this was not always the result of inadequate resources. GEC was content to accumulate a large cash mountain, relying almost exclusively upon its defence and telecommunications contracts. But for certain companies, in particular AEG, which recorded

Table 16   GEC's joint ventures, 1980-4

Company	Country	Product Area
Overseas companies considered for take-over		
ITT Europe	US	Telecommunications
STC	US/UK	Telecommunications
Stromberg Carlson	US	Telecommunications
United Tech	US	Electronics
Hughes Aircraft	US	Defence electronics
John Brown	US	Production engineering
ICL	UK	Computers
Inmos	UK	Microprocessors
AEG	Germany	Electronics
Mitel	Canada	Telecommunications

Company	Country	Production area
Collaboration entered into		
Mitsubishi	Japan	Satellites
NEC	Japan	Licence for cellular radio
Data General	US	Microcomputers
Xerox	US	Microcomputers
Communication Res.	US	Microcomputers
Intel	US	Microcomputers
Ferranti	UK	Anti-tank missile
Plessey	UK	System X exchange
Plessey	UK	Mobile radio
Pye	UK	Mobile radio
Air Call	UK	Mobile radio
AEG	Germany	Multi-launch rocket
Rheinmetall	Germany	Multi-launch rocket
Siemens	Germany	Telecoms components
Matra	France	Multi-launch rocket
Raytheon	France	Multi-launch rocket
Matra	France	Mobile radio
CIT-Alcatel	France	Telecommunications
Mitel	Canada	Licence for iso-CMOS

losses of DM 968m in 1979, and DM 278m in 1980, financing support did present a problem, causing external assistance to be sought. Accordingly, AEG, pursuing a cooperative rather than competitive strategy, concluded a licensing arrangement with the American

Table 17   AEG-Telefunken's joint ventures, acquisitions, and
disposals, 1980–4

Collaboration entered into		
Company	Country	Purpose
Mostek	US	Manufacture of ICs
JVC	Japan	Manufacture of VHS VCRs
Thorn EMI	UK	Manufacture of VHS VCRs
Bosch	Germany	Telematik project in IT
Mannesmann	Germany	Telematic project in IT

Acquisitions and investments		
Company	Country	Product area
Modular Computer	US	Civil and military computers
GEI-Gesellschaft	Germany	Software
DEBEG	Germany	Shipping communications

AEG also formed AEG-Telefunken Software-Technik Gmbh in order
to increase its share of the German software market.

Disposals		
Company	Country	Product area
H&B foreign subsidiaries	Germany	Electronics
Rosenthal Tech.	Germany	Electronics
ATN	Germany	TV station
Telefunken	Germany	Consumer electronics

company Mostek for the production of integrated circuits in
Europe, and turned to the German government along with the
European Commission for financial assistance (see Table 17).

From this brief analysis of selected IT companies, it is evident
that throughout the 1980s the forces of competition drove companies into forming collaborative alliances; government intervention or encouragement was not necessary. Furthermore, because
the majority of successful agreements appear to have been between European, American and Japanese companies, rather than

between British companies, or European companies alone, the economic, technological and strategic reasons for pursuing national, pre-competitive R&D programmes must be drawn into question.

A related factor concerns the extent to which the market, rather than technology, determines changes in strategy. For example, certain companies, because of the high level of very competitive Japanese imports, altered production away from consumer electronics and diversified into computers and telecommunications. In addition, the timing of a company's entry into a market, particularly one as complex and volatile as IT, can be of crucial importance in determining success: early entry may result in the company setting industry standards, but those entering at a later stage may avoid the pioneer's mistakes.

A further issue raised by this chapter concerns the role, if any, which the government ought to assume in encouraging or persuading companies to adopt particular strategies. Derek Roberts of GEC argued that the government's first concern ought to be with protecting the domestic industry, and he was particularly scornful of the British government's policy of encouraging inward investment, which he felt was merely subsidizing the establishment of Japanese subsidiaries, which would then be strategically well placed to avoid any subsequent trade restrictions.

> I wonder if anybody can name an industrial country which is exploiting tax payers' money to encourage foreign competitors in high technology areas to move into a country and fragment the market and competition. We have more fragmented our home markets with this country providing the money than the rest of Europe put together. I do believe one of the continuing political mistakes we have made is the unintelligent application of resources to encourage inward investment. (*House of Lords, op. cit.*)

A second requirement which European and British companies had of their governments was that they should be responsible for encouraging the adoption of European standards, thereby effectively creating a form of non-tariff barrier against Japanese imports. By erecting these entry barriers it was felt that the

European companies would be able to regain and maintain control of their domestic markets, and consequently would be in a much stronger position to bargain with the Americans and Japanese over technology exchanges together with licensing and marketing agreements. European companies thus appeared to be more concerned about the threat Japan posed to existing markets than about winning the Fifth Generation race.

7 Conclusion

This book, by reviewing the history of the IT industry, has attempted to describe and discuss those factors, both political and economical, which throughout the post-war period have contributed to the performance of certain companies and countries. We began this difficult and complex task by investigating the role national governments played in stimulating the early development of the computing and telecommunications industries. This was followed by an examination of the more recent Fifth Generation Computer initiatives in America, Japan, Britain and Europe. The last chapter analysed the strategies pursued throughout the early 1980s by a number of large European electronics companies.

The purpose of this final chapter is twofold: first, to investigate the interface between government and company strategies, and, second, to focus attention upon the importance of four central questions raised by the analysis.

The first question, which has been asked implicitly throughout the text, concerns the initiation of public assistance to industry, and whether the government or private companies ought to be responsible for instigating this support. Secondly, who is, or ought to be responsible for the framing and administering of government policies intended to assist companies? Thirdly, who benefits from such aid, and in what way? Finally, how does this aid distort the structure of the domestic industry, the strategies of individual companies, and the nature of international competition and trade patterns. Answers to these questions are of fundamental importance, not only in helping at least partially to explain inter-country differences in the development of the IT industry but also because, by providing a comparative assessment of governments' past and present roles in fostering and encouraging growth in this important area, they present a constructive and coherent list of remedies for effective government action in the future.

There is evidence to suggest that, whereas in Britain, Europe and the USA, government action designed to promote industrial development within the IT sector has generally been initiated by companies, in Japan the original stimulus has been largely generated by the government itself. MITI appears to be a more innovative institution than its European and American counterparts, assuming the role of strategic planner, advising and cajoling Japanese companies to pursue specific courses of development.

MITI's equivalent in the UK, the DTI, has pursued a considerably more passive role, relying upon appropriate policy suggestions from company representatives, via such bodies as the National Economic Development Council (NEDC) and the Advisory Council on Applied Research and Development (ACARD), rather than persuading companies to participate in a carefully planned, definite strategy. There are, however, a number of shortcomings inherent in the DTI's approach. First, there is the grave and ever-present danger that the larger companies will be over-represented in such forums, and that as a consequence government policy will reflect the interests of such companies, possibly to the exclusion of those which are smaller and medium-sized. Furthermore, it could be argued that large companies, even without the aid of quangos giving them direct access to the corridors of Whitehall power, by virtue of their size, are already strategically well positioned to influence the government.

Secondly, and of equal importance, is the danger that advice the government receives from companies will be geared towards improvements (for those companies) in the short term rather than the medium or long term. It has been said that as far as strategic planning is concerned, three years ahead is as far as any company is prepared to look, whereas within MITI plans are usually made with a decade of change in mind.

Thirdly, the advice received by the government via these channels will be conservative and largely defensive of the *status quo*, since large companies are unlikely to suggest that competition-stimulating innovation would result if they were either split up, or in some way restricted.

Finally, because the approach adopted by the DTI has resulted in the government relying upon the advice of large established companies, it is possible that new developments in smaller companies, often working in emerging fields, may fail to receive appropriate public support, resulting in an unsuccessful sharpening of the competitive edge as funds continue to be channelled into traditional areas. This can be particularly dangerous in the ever-changing market for consumer electronics goods (see Figure 7).

These problems, stemming from the British approach, apply equally to the European Community. Because the ESPRIT programme lacked a firm base of support from within the Council of Ministers, the Commission turned to the leading European electronics companies for assistance, and accordingly ESPRIT became an embodiment of the interests of twelve large companies.

Although not widely publicized, numerous Japanese companies are opposed to MITI's policies, and actively campaign against the implementation of its recommendations, many of which are seen as being, while possibly to the advantage of the country's long-term industrial future, against their short-term individual interests. This was to a certain extent the case with both the VLSI research programme in 1976 and the Fifth Generation Project in 1981.

Despite the fact that America has had little in the way of official industrial policies, the DoD has had a long history of initiating policies, in particular the provision of lucrative defence contracts, many of which have had the effect of giving an advantage to her domestic electronics industry. It has been argued by many companies that this 'trade' rather than 'aid' approach (usually to be

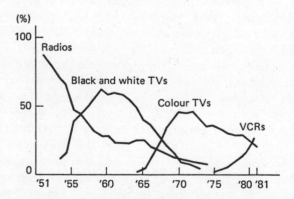

Figure 7 Composition ratio trends in the production of major consumer electronics equipment (consumer electronics equipment total = 100 per cent)

Source: MITI, *Statistics on Production Trend*, 1982 (partly revised).

found in the development context) provides the most satisfactory form of assistance which the government can give to industry.

In Britain since 1979 the influence of increased MoD spending has had the effect of stimulating the defence electronics industry, but in a rather less favourable way. Whereas in the USA support for the defence electronics industry has tended to lead, through subcontracts, to renewed and revitalized developments in other sectors of the electronics industry, in Britain efforts have been diverted away from other sectors and concentrated almost exclusively upon defence. Indeed, such has been the profitability of the closed market defence sector for Britain's largest electronics firms that attempts to pioneer innovations in the sphere of business and commerce, where the return on capital investments is lower, and overseas competition, in a relatively open market, is extremely fierce, have frequently been abandoned.

One of the principal arguments for government intervention in the IT industry, in the countries studied, has rested upon the need to protect the domestic industry from the competitive advantage enjoyed by rivals already receiving and benefiting from considerable government support. For example, the heavy investment by the DoD in the US semiconductor industry during the 1960s and 1970s, gave American companies, including Texas Instruments and Intel, an important competitive edge, which, in the absence of similar assistance, other countries seemed unlikely to erode. However, a challenge to this American hegemony was beginning to emerge from Japan.

The Japanese government, by developing the concept of collaborative, pre-competitive R&D between private electronics companies, effectively matched the American effort at a fraction of the cost. Although MITI's attempts in the early 1970s to restructure the Japanese electronics industry at the marketing and product level were largely unsuccessful, the collaborative R&D programme into VLSI in 1976–80 was an unprecedented success. By the beginning of the 1980s, as a consequence of pooling the resources of its manufacturers, MITI managed to push the Japanese semiconductor industry ahead of its American counterpart without sustaining the massive financial cost of the American procurement policy of the 1960s and 1970s.

The success of this Japanese initiative spurred Europe into action on the following basis: if the Japanese can leapfrog the Americans with only the minimum of government financial assistance (though with a large measure of direction and consensus building), so can we. Early in the 1980s, given that the recession had greatly reduced the ability of European governments to inject public funds into domestic industries, IT was considered to be an area where, provided a coherent, collaborative research programme, involving companies, universities and government bodies, in pursuit of common aims was established, value for money could be almost guaranteed.

However, whereas the Japanese had focused their activities on very specific, clearly achievable objectives, the British and Europeans, in a burst of over-enthusiasm and over-confidence, missed the essence of the Japanese lesson, and failed to specify definite, realistically attainable goals, having programmes designed to cover virtually the whole spectrum of advanced computer technology. Despite this, the British and European programmes did, to a certain extent, influence the strategies of major British and European electronics companies, by encouraging inter-company contact and cooperation, which senior members of both the Alvey and ESPRIT directorates hoped would extend beyond the R&D stage, leading perhaps to a cartelized European electronics industry, strongly placed to meet the challenge of international competition.

Although both the Alvey and ESPRIT directorates remained optimistic about the possibility of genuine long-term collaboration extending to production and marketing, in reality it appeared to be the case that European companies were willing to cooperate with each other only in the area of R&D, and were more interested in concluding production and marketing agreements with Japanese and American companies. For example, Olivetti finalized such contracts with both AT&T of America and Toshiba of Japan, thereby successfully uniting Olivetti's computer and office automation with AT&T's telecommunication experience and Toshiba's strength in consumer electronics. By forging such global coalitions between companies which may not be in direct competition with one another, each company can simultaneously increase both its product range and distribution network.

The analysis of this chapter has so far suggested that governments ought to adopt a policy of selective assistance towards the IT industry. Instead of trying unsuccessfully to support every aspect of a complex, fiercely competitive and rapidly changing industry, resources would be employed more effectively and profitably if channelled into one area of specialization, so that each country could play a valuable role in a global coalition.

Both Alvey and ESPRIT are compromises, the results of having allowed industry, with its diversity of interests, too influential a role in the planning of government programmes, and as a consequence the whole process has reduced to a mere money-sharing exercise. At present, in Britain, the Alvey Programme has been held up as evidence that the government is taking a leading role in promoting the UK IT industry, when in fact it is not leading but following: the suggestions have all been made by dominant companies of the IT community, thereby negating the influence of public support and raising serious questions about whether anything 'additional' is being done as a direct consequence of the programme.

This is not to say that national governments do not have any role to play in assisting their IT industries; they do, since by controlling direct and indirect financial and non-financial market-distorting aid, including tariffs, taxes, education, research grants, national standards and procurement policies, they are to a certain extent, responsible for creating the climate and environment within which industries operate. Consequently, though by introducing their own distortions, governments do have an important role to play in helping companies surmount these market imperfections.

Throughout the analysis of the Japanese, US, European and British IT industries, two particularly important governmental issues have prevailed. The first concerns the controversy between the supporters of free trade and the supporters of protectionism. On balance the major British and European electronics companies have tended to favour liberalization, both within Europe to promote a large EEC market, and internationally to end the free ride of protectionist Japan. The second issue concerns the debate about the introduction of common international standards. Throughout the post-war period, because individual countries have been reluctant to abandon hopes of their national champion becoming the standard setter, and because of ambivalence over the possibility of success without the participation of IBM, who refused to make its own standards open, Europe has found concluding agreements on the details of standards to be a particularly long and difficult process. However, one of the major spin-offs of the ESPRIT programme was that it helped push Europe closer to having established common IT standards. Sir Herbert Durking of Plessey commented:

> One of the by-products of ESPRIT which in some ways has perhaps been the most successful is the standardization aspect. All the companies involved have agreed to accept a set of standards, which are called open system interconnect standards, and work towards these ... CEPT and CENLEC are now active in promoting these standards. (*House of Lords, op. cit.*)

The interface between government and the IT industry in Britain and Europe is complicated. Europe and Britain are clearly both at a competitive disadvantage compared with the ability of the Americans and, particularly, the Japanese to construct and execute public policies, and this has led certain experts to argue that the European and British governments should, in an attempt to limit the wasteful disposal of taxpayers' money, do the bare minimum for the IT industry. But this is not to say that the government should do nothing at all. What the government must appreciate is, firstly that IT is a global industry, one in which coalitions with American and Japanese companies ought to be encouraged; and secondly, that direct cash contributions to companies are likely to be less effective than a coherent policy of infrastructural support. We feel that the latter would be best developed by a team of qualified and experienced civil servants, who may be better positioned to have a long-term view of the British IT industry than industrialists working within it.

Bibliography

ABRC, *Review of R&D in the UK*, HMSO, 1982.

ACARD, *Information Technology*, HMSO, September 1980.

ALVEY COMMITTEE, *A Programme for Advanced Information Technology: The Report of the Alvey Committee*, HMSO, 1983.

ALVEY DIRECTORATE, *Alvey Programme Annual Report 1984*, DTI/IEE, 1984.

ALVEY DIRECTORATE, *Alvey Programme Annual Report 1985*, DTI/IEE, 1985.

ARNOLD, ERIK, 'A Preliminary Comparison of IT Programmes: A Report to the Alvey Directorate', mimeo, SPRU, March 1985.

BORRUS, MICHAEL et al., *The Impacts of Divestiture and Deregulation: Infrastructure Changes, Manufacturing Transition and Competition in the US Telecommunications Industry*, Project for the US Congress Office of Technology Assessment, September 1984.

BRADY, TIM, 'Which is Which?: A Guide to Public Body Investment in Information Technology in the UK', mimeo, SPRU, April 1983.

BRAUN, ERNEST and MACDONALD, STUART, *Revolution in Miniature: The History and Impact of Semiconductor Electronics*, CUP, 1978.

CAGLAR, LEVENT et al., 'Technology Transfer from University to Industry: The Problem in Britain', *Creativity and Innovation Network*, January 1983.

CARTER, SIR CHARLES (ed.), *Industrial Policy and Innovation*, Heinemann, 1981.

COOMBS, ROB; SAVIOTTI, PAOLO, and WALSH, VIVIEN, *Technological Innovation Economics and Public Policy*, Macmillan, 1985.

DOSI, GIOVANNI, *Technological Change and Industrial Transformation: The Theory and an Application to the Semiconductor Industry*, Macmillan, 1984.

ENGLISH, MAURICE and WATSON-BROWNE, ADAM, 'National Policies in Information Technology: Challenges and Responses', *Oxford Surveys in Information Technology*, vol. 1, 1985.

EUROPEAN COMMISSION, *Proposal for a Council Decision: Adopting the First European Strategic Programme for Research & Development in Information Technology*, 2 June 1983, COM(83)FINAL.

EUROPEAN COMMISSION, *Proposal for a European Scientific and Technical Strategy Framework Programme 1984–87*, 1982, COM(82)865.

FEIGENBAUM, EDWARD, A. and McCORDUCK, PAMELA, *The Fifth Generation: Artificial Intelligence and Japan's Computer Challenge to the World*, Michael Joseph, 1984.

FORESTER, TOM (ed.), *The Microelectronics Revolution*, Basil Blackwell, 1980.

FREEMAN, CHRISTOPHER *et al.*, *Unemployment and Technological Innovation*, Frances Pinter, 1982.

HAY, D. A., and MORRIS, D. J., *Industrial Economics*, OUP, 1979.

HEERTIE, ARNOLD, *Economics and Technical Change*: Weidenfeld & Nicholson, 1977.

HILLS, JILL, *Information Technology and Industrial Policy*, Croom Helm, 1984.

HOUSE OF LORDS, *University–Industry Relations*, HMSO, October 1976.

HOUSE OF LORDS, *ESPRIT*, HMSO, 1985.

LANDS, FRANK, 'Information Technology: The Alvey Report and Government Strategy', Inaugural lecture, LSE, 1 March 1983, mimeo LSE.

MACKENZIE, IAN, and HESSELMAN, LINDA, 'European Electronics in an Era of US–Japanese Competition', Paper presented to a conference at Chatham House, mimeo, London Business School, November 1984.

MACKINTOSH, IAN, 'A Survey of Community Support Programmes and Strategies in Information Technology', Paper presented at Brussels, Esprit Technical Week, 1984.

MADDOCK, SIR IEUAN, Civil Exploitation of Defence Technology, Report to Electronics EDC and Observations of the Ministry of Defence, NEDO, 1983.

MIDDLEMAS, KEITH, *Industry, Unions, and Government: Twenty-one Years of NEDC*, Macmillan, 1984.

OECD, *The Future of University Research*, March, 1981.

OECD, *Science and Technology Indicators: Resources Devoted to R&D*, 1984.

OFFICE OF TECHNOLOGY ASSESSMENT (US CONGRESS), *International Competitiveness in Electronics*, Washington, DC, November 1983.

OKIMOTO, DANIEL *et al.* (eds), *Competitive Edge: The Semiconductor Industry in the US and Japan*, Stanford University Press, 1984.

PACTEL: *A Strategy for IT*, August 1981.

REDWOOD, JOHN, *Going for Broke*, Basil Blackwell, 1985.

ROSENBURG, NATHAN, *Inside the Black Box: Technology and Economics*, CUP, 1982.

ROTHWELL, ROY, and ZEGFELD, WALTER. *Innovation and the Small and Medium Sized Firm*, Frances Pinter, 1981.

ROTHWELL, ROY, and ZEGFELD, WALTER, *Industrial Innovation and Public Policy*, Frances Pinter, 1981.

SAWYER, MALCOLM C., *Theories of the Firm*, Weidenfeld & Nicolson, 1979.

SAWYER, MALCOLM C., *The Economics of Industry and Firms,* Croom Helm, 1981.

SCIBERRAS, EDMUND, *Multinational Electronics Companies and National Economic Policies,* JAI Press, 1977.

SCOTT, J., *An Economic Theory of Business Strategy,* Martin Robertson, 1981.

ZYSMAN, J. and TYSON, L., 'US and Japanese Trade and Industrial Policies', mimeo, Berkeley, California, September 1984.

Index

99